Scots
cooking

Former BBC Masterchef and winner of the *Sunday Times* Amateur Chef of the Year award, Sue Lawrence wrote recipes for the *Sunday Times* from 1993 to 1999 and is the author of eight cookery books, including *On Baking*. She has contributed articles to a range of national piblications, from *Sainsbury's The Magazine* to *Country Living*, and writes a column in *Scotland on Sunday*. She regularly appears on television and radio talking about scottish cookery.

Sue was born in Dundee and raised in Edinburgh, then spent a period moving about Europe with her pilot husband. They returned to Edinburgh in 1989, where they live with their three children.

Also by Sue Lawrence

Scots
cooking

The best traditional
and contemporary
Scottish recipes

SUE LAWRENCE

HEADLINE

In memory of my dear friend Fiona

First published in 2000
by HEADLINE BOOK PUBLISHING

First published in paperback in 2002
by HEADLINE BOOK PUBLISHING

10 9 8 7 6 5 4 3 2 1

ISBN 0 7472 7126 7

Edited by Jane Middleton
Art directed by Ellen Wheeler
Designed by Town
Photography by Marie-Louise Avery
Food styling by Jacqueline Clarke

Printed and bound in Italy by
Canale and C. S.p.A

HEADLINE BOOK PUBLISHING
A division of the Hodder Headline Group
338 Euston Road
London NW1 3BH

www.headline.co.uk
www.hodderheadline.com

Acknowledgements

I should like to thank my parents for delving into the past to recall what they ate some 60 or 70 years ago. Also, my sister Carol for her invaluable help researching Arbroath recipes; and my dear aunts, Muriel and Bette, for remembrance of things past – and for my grandmother's recipe book.

As ever, I am eternally grateful to my family's tastebuds: thank you, Pat, Euan, Faith and Jessica for being (occasionally unwilling!) guinea pigs.

Special thanks to Catherine Brown for the inspiration I have received from her splendid books. And to Clarissa Dickson Wright and Joanna Blythman for their unfailing support, encouragement and friendship.

And to the following people for helping to make it happen

Kenny Adamson, baker, Pittenweem

Robin Adamson, University of Dundee

Catherine and Roddy Aflin, Stornoway, Isle of Lewis

Gavin Borthwick and Christine McFarlane at George Armstrong, fishmonger, Edinburgh

Lady Buccleuch, Drumlanrig Castle

Clark Brothers, fishmongers, Musselburgh

Joan Bunting, Gosforth, Newcastle

Herbert Cox, The Seafield Hotel, Cullen

David Craig, Robertson's Butcher, Broughty Ferry

Guy Craig, Udny Arms, Aberdeenshire

Audrey Dyer and Alec Smith at George Bower, Butcher, Edinburgh

David Goodfellow, Goodfellow & Steven, Dundee and Broughty Ferry

Alison and Ian Gray, Edinburgh

Sue and Frank Hadden, Edinburgh

Simon Hopkinson, London

Margaret Horn, The But 'n' Ben, Auchmithie

Caroline Keith, Scottish Tourist Board

Anthony Laing, Shortbread House of Edinburgh

Fred and Moira MacAulay, Perth

Dods Macfarlane, Isle of Lewis

Aggie MacKenzie, Rothiemurchus

Mackie family, Mackie's Ice-cream, Aberdeenshire

Iain Macleod, butcher, Stornoway, Isle of Lewis

Rhoda Macleod, Isle of Harris

Jo, Kate and John Macsween, Edinburgh

Arthur McDonald, of the Crofting Township Development Scheme

Angela McKenzie, pastry chef, Peebles Hydro

Alan McPherson, The Seafield Bakery, Cullen

Effie Morrison, Isle of Harris

Grace Mulligan, North Humberside

Ramsay of Carluke, Lanarkshire

Tom Rodger, Aberfeldy Water Mill

Rosemary Shrager, Amhuinnsuidhe, Isle of Harris

Alec Smith, Arbroath

Hamish Taylor, Isle of Harris

Carol and Jim Tollerton, Arbroath

Beverley Tricker, Aberdeen and Grampian Tourist Board

Georgia Wishart, Shetland

Martin Wishart, Restaurant Martin Wishart, Edinburgh

Linda Wood, Tarbert

John Young, Breadalbane Bakery, Aberfeldy

Contents

Introduction

'We don't always eat chips. Sometimes we leave them overnight and eat them cold next day – and that's what in Scotland we call a salad.'

This riposte on Radio 4's 'News Quiz' by Scottish comedian Fred MacAulay certainly made everyone laugh. But, sad to say, there is more than a hint of truth in it. The words 'healthy diet' and 'Scotland' have not often been uttered in the same breath. And with one of the worst records for heart disease in the world, it was not before time when health boards recently began to look critically at Scotland's diet. And what a lot of chips they found.

But it was not always thus. Chips only came to Scotland at the turn of the century. Indeed, many of the traditional dishes that have been saved from extinction are exceedingly healthy, provided they are not supplemented by commercial cakes or pappy white bread. And provided everything is not deep-fried in batter.

Consider the mainstays of the Scots diet over the centuries: oatcakes, porridge, Scotch broth and herring. Oats are one of those super-healthy foods that we are advised to eat more of because of their good soluble fibre, iron, zinc and vitamins. Broths bulging with barley and vegetables retain many health-giving minerals and vitamins, instead of being boiled away to nothing or, worse, tipped down the sink in the vegetable-boiling water. And herring and other oily fish such as salmon are well known for their health-giving properties because of their omega-3 fatty acids, which can help prevent both cancer and heart disease.

If, therefore, we went 'back to basics' instead of embracing every new processed or takeaway food on offer, we would be an exceedingly healthy nation indeed. And since there are those in Scotland who wish to 'rise and be a nation again', why not start by returning to the old – and undoubtedly healthier – diet?

As I looked through old books while researching recipes, I was interested – and, I must say, surprised – by the variety of foods on offer throughout the centuries. Sadly, much of this variety was confined to the big houses, to the aristocratic and grand families who could afford servants to bleed their hares and pluck their pheasants. Theirs was a diet that included copious breakfasts of porridge, oat or barley bannocks, conserves and cured fish. Lunch ('dinner') was soup, such as barley broth, partan bree or cock-a-leekie, followed by some sort of meat or fowl, boiled or roasted or served in a pie. Until Victorian times, when *service à la russe* (individual courses) became popular, puddings and sweets were served with the second course, beside the roasts. So you might have a lemon 'hatted-kit' (junket) or 'sillie bub' served at the same time as the roast kid or hare ragout. Supper was similar, with perhaps some lighter dishes such as eggs or fish.

But for poorer people, the diet was less diverse. And although it was plain, possibly mundane, there was nothing wrong with it, for it was honest, simple fare that sustained men and women for centuries, whatever their lot. My parents ate mince and tatties several times a week during their childhood, with little except broth and porridge at other meals. But they did not complain, for it was good and wholesome. Nothing fancy. Fancy food, such as cloutie dumpling or black bun, was for special occasions like birthdays and Hogmanay.

In previous centuries, breakfast for the average unprivileged person would have been porridge or brose, followed by broth for dinner (fish based if they were near the sea) and an evening meal of root vegetables such as turnips or potatoes and kail with oatcakes or bannocks – with milk if they had cattle. In less fertile areas and in times of shortage, the proportion of dairy food would have been higher. Martin Martin, writing in 1703 in *A Description of the Western Islands of Scotland*, tells of the people of Skye's 'ordinary diet': there was butter, milk, cheese, potatoes and brochan (oatmeal boiled with water). For poor Highlanders and Lowlanders, meat was a luxury that was seldom enjoyed, except at special festivities. Or, if there were 'casualties' among the herds of cows, sheep or goats, people would use the entire animal to make black puddings, white puddings, sheep's head broth, goat hams and pickled mutton, which would last for months. Shetland's famous reestit (reested) mutton is still very much in demand before Christmas, the traditional time for killing and preserving the beasts.

Those poorer people who lived near the sea would eat shellfish that we now think of as a luxury. Oysters, crabs and lobsters were everyday fare. Salmon was so plentiful that farm workers used to stipulate that they did not want to eat it more than twice a week. There is a lovely tale of a Highland gentleman visiting London in the early 1800s and ordering beef steak for himself and salmon for his servant, since in Scotland the fish was so cheap. He was surprised to discover that his own meal cost mere pence and his servant's several shillings. Seaweed was also used – and indeed still is by people living beside the sea – in soups and stews. One such person is Margaret Horn from Auchmithie, who was brought up on plain fare such as grilled dulse, Scotch broth and boiled lobster before the latter became a luxury.

In all the references to Scots meals and food throughout literature, whether it is the critical Samuel Johnson commenting on the pre-breakfast dram in 1773, the more cheerful Dorothy Wordsworth writing in 1803 about oat bread and blue-milk cheese for breakfast, or Tom Steel describing the St Kildans' pre-evacuation life in 1930 with their fulmar brose and puffin-flavoured porridge, there is one overriding sentiment noted by all visitors, and that is hospitality. For however we may enjoy the 'You'll have had your tea' jokes, there is little doubt that Scots are renowned for their hospitality. Whether with a dram and a piece of 'shortie' or a cup of tea and a scone, visitors are always welcomed to the home. Offering food and drink plays an integral part.

While this warmth and conviviality have – hopefully – not altered over the centuries, our eating habits have. Perhaps instead of resorting to pre-packed processed meals laden with preservatives and unnecessary additives we could return to the honest ingredients raised and grown on our soil and treat them with the respect they were accorded in days of dire poverty. Then perhaps we would realise that true Scots cooking is good. It is simple and healthy, unintimidating and unpretentious, accessible to everyone, rich and poor. Even non-Scots can understand the sentiment, if not all the words, in this verse from Burns' famous poem about egalitarianism, 'A Man's a Man for a' That', written in 1795, shortly after the French Revolution (with which Burns sympathised):

'What though on hamely fare we dine
Wear hoddin grey and a' that
Gie fools their silks and knaves their wine
A Man's a Man for a' that.'

There has never been anything wrong with homely fare. Let us revisit our roots, return to natural ingredients, eschew unhealthy processed foods and remember that Scots cooking means simple, honest – and, most importantly – good food.

Sue Lawrence

breakfast and preserves

'Not long after the dram, may be expected the breakfast, a meal in which the Scots, whether of the Lowlands or mountains, must be confessed to excel us. The tea and coffee are accompanied not only with butter, but with honey, conserves and marmalades. If an epicure could remove by a wish, in quest of sensual gratifications, wherever he had supped he would breakfast in Scotland.'

Thus spake Dr Samuel Johnson during his voyage around Scotland with James Boswell in 1773. Praise indeed from a man who disparaged much of the country's diet throughout the tour, particularly the Scots' staple, oats. But apart from the tea, coffee, honey, conserves and porridge, let us not forget the black pudding, Lorne sausage, Ayrshire bacon and eggs. Or ham 'n' haddie, hot-buttered Arbroath smokie or grilled finnan haddock – with barley or oat bannocks, oatcakes, butteries and baps on the side.

I have to agree with Dr Johnson about Scotland being the perfect place for breakfast, provided it is proper porridge (made slowly with salt and water, never milk) and local ingredients judiciously cooked to provide that essential first meal of the day, which we now know should be wholesome, sustaining and hearty. I also find myself concurring with his opinion about an old-fashioned dish offered to him in the Hebrides. James Boswell tells the lady of the house he does not think the Doctor will accept sheep's head for breakfast, but she offers it anyway:

> '"Do you choose any cold sheep's-head, sir?"
>
> "No, madam," said he with a tone of surprise and anger.
>
> "It is here, sir," said she, supposing he had refused it to save the trouble of bringing it in.
>
> They thus went on at cross purposes, till he confirmed his refusal in a manner not to be misunderstood; while I sat quietly by and enjoyed my success.'

I wonder what he would have thought about the rice crispies and soggy white toast on offer in many establishments providing so-called Scottish breakfasts today. I think even he might opt for sheep's head instead.

Breakfast Pancakes

My cousin Frank is hardly ever in the kitchen, so busy is his working day. But Sunday morning is sacred, for this is when he cooks the family pancakes for breakfast. He follows a tight routine, which alters little from one week to the next. First he gets up half an hour before everyone else and begins to prepare the batter. Once the first pancake is cooking, it is time to separate the Sunday papers into 'reading' and 'bin'. Then, once the rest of the family has been called – and Frank's younger son, Scott, has devoured at least six pancakes – Frank allows himself the last two, with melted butter, golden syrup, lime juice and brown sugar. The only other essential accompaniment is the sports supplement of the paper. The rest has in all probability landed in the bin.

Makes 12–15

300g/10½oz flour (either plain or self-raising; use whatever you have to hand)
2 large free-range eggs, beaten
500ml/18fl oz semi-skimmed milk
a pinch of salt
1 tablespoon melted butter, plus extra to serve
golden syrup, lime juice and soft brown sugar, to serve

Sift the flour into a bowl and mix in the eggs with a fork. Add the milk and, using a hand-held electric mixer, beat until the batter is smooth. Add the salt and a third of the melted butter, folding them in to combine.

Heat a pancake pan (a regular 20cm/8in crêpe pan) and lightly smear the base with some of the remaining melted butter, using a wad of kitchen paper. Leave to heat up for a couple of minutes, then pour in a small ladleful – or 1½ tablespoons – of the batter and swirl it around the base. Cook over a medium heat for about 40 seconds, until it no longer looks raw, then flip it over. (Frank tosses each pancake ceilingwards unless he has a hangover.) Cook the other side, which should take no more than 30 seconds. (It is time to begin sorting out the Sunday papers.)

Remove the pancake, smear the pan lightly with more butter and cook the remaining pancakes. Depending on the reliability of the pan, you might not need to smear it every time. The pancakes can be piled up on a plate to keep warm while you make the rest. Serve with melted butter, golden syrup, lime juice and soft brown sugar.

Porridge

'Halesome parritch, chief o' Scotia's food,' wrote Burns, Scotland's great bard. And surely Burns, with his keen sense of irony, would have found it exceedingly amusing to discover that, over 200 years later, Scotland's humblest dish was the height of fashion. London's latest eating places cannot make enough porridge to satisfy their eager customers. The white chocolate, banana and cinnamon toppings might have offended the purist in him but he was, after all, known for his liberal views.

Ever since polenta – north Italy's peasant maize porridge – became hugely fashionable during the 1990s, our own oatmeal porridge has been long overdue for a comeback. Not that it ever went away for most Scots. When I was a child, porridge was cooked for breakfast every single day, summer and winter. My sister and I took our porridge in the Sassenach way, with brown sugar and top of the milk drizzled over it – or rather, the milk was poured around the sides, moat-like. But when my parents were children, they ate it in the traditional Scottish way: hot porridge was ladled into bowls (usually wooden) and a smaller bowl containing milk placed alongside. Then, with your spoon (usually horn), you took a spoonful of porridge, dipped it into the milk bowl and ate it. This meant the porridge stayed hot and the milk cold longer. It was only embellished with salt, never sugar. Porridge was, interestingly, always referred to as 'they' – and 'they' were traditionally eaten standing up, never seated.

F. Marian McNeill's recipe for porridge is one that many people still use. Instead of soaking the oatmeal overnight and cooking it the next day, she recommended that it should be slowly released through the fingers of a clenched fist while stirring madly with the spurtle (also called a theevil) – the long wooden stick used specifically for porridge. Polenta is, of course, made in the same way and the *bastone* – polenta-stirrer – is also a long wooden stick.

And just as polenta is cooked, cooled then fried or grilled, so is porridge: porridge would be ladled into the drawer of a kitchen dresser (called a kist in the north-east of Scotland) and left to cool. Once solid, it was cut and taken into the hills as sustenance for a hard day's work. In the evening, slices (called calders) were cut off to be fried and served with eggs or fish.

But it is at breakfast that porridge has always been the star attraction, whether you adhere rigidly to the salt-only dogma or top with brown sugar and cream. It is recorded that on the now uninhabited island of St Kilda, 'breakfast normally consisted of porridge and milk, with a puffin boiled in with the oats to give flavour'. Each to their own.

To Dr Samuel Johnson's remark that oats were a 'grain, which in England is generally given to horses but in Scotland supports the people' came the marvellous riposte by a Scot, Lord Elibank: 'And where will you get such men and such horses?' A bowl of porridge is indeed the most healthy and delicious breakfast possible. Enjoy them!

Traditionally oatmeal is used for porridge. If you are using rolled or porridge oats (which have far less flavour than oatmeal as they are already steamed or part-cooked), you will need 1 cup of oats to about 2½ cups of water and you can reduce the cooking time below to 3–4 minutes. Medium oatmeal is the most commonly used but I prefer coarse. Pinhead makes a nice change, with its pronounced nubbly texture.

Serves 3–4
1 cup of medium, coarse or pinhead oatmeal
about 3 cups of cold water
a good pinch of salt

Put the oatmeal in a pan with the water and leave to soak overnight. Next day, add the salt and bring slowly to the boil. Stirring frequently – preferably with a spurtle – cook for about 10 minutes (about 15 minutes for pinhead oatmeal) over a medium to low heat, until thick and creamy. Serve at once.

Brose

Brose is an acquired taste. Having been brought up on porridge, I found it difficult to enjoy brose at first, especially since butter is added with the salt, but then I remembered that butter was stirred into the oat, barley and rice porridges I enjoyed in Finland during the year I spent there. The addition of butter seemed to make the oatmeal even smoother. If you don't like the butter, just dip spoonfuls of the brose into milk or cream, or even douse it with sugar, syrup or treacle if you prefer. But do not do this anywhere near a 'brosie' person, which is old Scots dialect for 'fed with brose'.

One such person is Ian Gray, an Aberdonian now living in Edinburgh, who has eaten brose almost every day of his life. He likes the texture to be smooth, although some prefer it 'knotty' – with lumps, the insides of which should contain raw oatmeal. Ian's father, from Buchan, not only likes knotty brose, he also adds pepper to his morning bowlful. And Evelyn Stevens from Caithness recommends brose for poor stomachs. As a child, as well as her daily oatmeal brose she also had peasemeal brose, made of milled roasted dried peas, which is typical in certain areas, particularly the north-east.

Flavourings such as honey, sugar or dried fruit can be added to brose. But the St Kildan habit of pouring the stock from a boiled fulmar over oatmeal to make a simple breakfast brose is unique; the St Kildans believed it to be good for the stomach. There is a Hebridean recipe for brose made with cream, not water, in which the cream is mixed directly with the dry oatmeal. Boiling beef stock or buttermilk is also sometimes used instead of boiling water.

Brochan, a thin oatmeal gruel, is taken instead of brose in certain areas. And sowens, another type of brose or porridge, is an alternative. It is made by soaking the mealy husks of the ground oats in a tub of water for several days until they begin to ferment, then this is sieved and boiled with water and salt to produce a thin porridge similar in texture to brochan. According to F. Marian McNeill, sowens cooked with butter was a traditional Hallowe'en dish; a ring was placed in it and whoever got the ring would be the first to marry.

She also describes in detail the method of making brose: 'Put into a bowl two handfuls of oatmeal. Add salt and a piece of butter. Pour in boiling water to cover the oatmeal and stir it up roughly with the shank of a horn spoon, allowing it to form knots. Sup with soor dook [buttermilk] or sweet milk, and you have a dish that has been the backbone of many a sturdy Scotsman.'

It was, however, only certain sturdy Scotsmen and women who would take brose in the mornings – primarily single men living in bothies (rough huts used as living accommodation for unmarried farm workers) and also cottars who lived in the farmer's tied cottages. Since they were often paid in kind with farm produce such as oatmeal, it made sense to cook and eat it. The staple diet of these farm workers would have been primarily milk, tatties and meal, with brose eaten at least twice a day. It was surely one of the earliest forms of fast food. And because the oatmeal was uncooked, it did not swell as much as porridge, so a person was capable of consuming an inordinate amount in one dish – anything up to 350g/12oz, which would have made 8–10 bowls of porridge! It is little wonder that traditionally men stood to eat breakfast; sitting down might have proved painful. Nowadays it is only in certain north-eastern and Hebridean areas and parts of Fife that the brose habit persists, unlike porridge which is popular throughout Scotland.

Serves 1
2 tablespoons medium oatmeal
a pinch of salt
a small knob of butter

Warm a bowl slightly (I place it in a low oven for 10 minutes or so as I pad about the kitchen, coming to in the morning with the first of many mugs of tea). Place the oatmeal in the bowl with the salt and butter. Pour over enough boiling water to form a fairly stiff, yet soft consistency – anything from 7–10 tablespoons. Stir well, then continue stirring until smooth. Eat dipped into milk.

Lorne Sausage and Egg

Lorne sausage is a square sausage made of beef. Although there can be some decidedly grim offerings that are far too greasy, a well-made Lorne sausage is sublime. David Craig of Robertson's Butcher's in Broughty Ferry prepares his with a minimum of 75 per cent beef. It makes a wonderfully satisfying breakfast – especially if you do as many Scots do and cram the sausage into a soft morning roll, with or without an egg. You are unlikely to encounter this joyful gastronomic treat in luxury hotel dining rooms but go on any of the Caledonian Macbrain ferries (Calmac to the passengers) to the islands and this – preceded by a mighty bowl of porridge – will greet you on the morning runs. Come rain, hail or shine.

Serves 1
2 slices of Lorne sausage (if you slice it yourself, cut it fairly thickly)
1 large free-range egg

Heat a reliable heavy frying pan until very hot, then add the Lorne sausage (without fat) and fry for 2–3 minutes before checking to see if a good crust has formed underneath. If so, turn over and continue to fry for 2–3 minutes, until cooked through. Meanwhile, fry the egg in the fat that has come out of the sausage. If you feel you need more fat, add a drop or two of oil.

To serve, eat as it is or place the sausage and egg in a large morning roll (lightly buttered) and devour with a mug of tea all by yourself, so that no one need comment on the juices and egg yolk dripping down your chin.

Black Pudding with Ayrshire Bacon

There are many variations on black pudding throughout Scotland but only one traditional Ayrshire bacon. Like Wiltshire bacon, it is brine-cured, but whereas Wiltshire bacon sides are cured with the rind on and bones in, the Ayrshire sides have the rind off and bones out. Ayrshire bacon became a by-product of dairy farming (the whey being fed to pigs) many centuries ago. Ramsay of Carluke is probably the only butcher's that cures its meat by hand in the traditional way from start to finish. The pigs are skinned, then boned, trimmed, cured, matured, rolled and either smoked or left green. The typical breakfast cut is Ayrshire middle, which Andrew Ramsay calls frying bacon. The fat on his bacon is firm and white and the flesh bright; the taste is good old-fashioned real food.

As for the black pudding, every butcher seems to have a different recipe. I am particularly fond of one from the Isle of Lewis. Iain Macleod of Charles Macleod's Butchers (known locally as Charley Barley's) in Stornoway sells a wonderful pudding made primarily of sheep's blood and oatmeal. It has a lovely crumbly, moist texture and a true, mutton-like flavour. He has never divulged the exact recipe to me but it is similar to those puddings still made at home in the Hebrides. Lewis-born Rhoda Macleod let me into the secret of her recipe for *marag dubh* (Gaelic for black pudding) which is simply 2 cups of oatmeal, 1 of flour, 2 of suet, 2 of onions and enough sheep's blood to give a dropping consistency.

At John Henderson's butcher's in Kircaldy, black pudding is made from lamb's blood, pork fat, cloves and nutmeg. He describes this as Scottish black pudding, as it has finely shredded pork fat throughout, instead of the larger chunks of fat typical of most English puddings and French *boudins*.

Serve this wonderfully simple breakfast dish with a fried egg, grilled tomatoes and plenty of hot buttered toast.

Serves 2
6 slices of Ayrshire middle bacon
4 thick slices of black pudding

Cook the bacon for 2–3 minutes in a hot frying pan (without extra fat), then turn it over and push to one side. You should now have enough bacon fat in the pan to fry your black pudding. If not, add a tiny knob of butter. Add the black pudding slices and cook for 4–5 minutes (depending on thickness), turning once, or until crisp on each side and cooked through. Serve at once on warm plates.

Butteries

It was half-past midnight as I strolled down the road to The Seafield Bakery in Cullen. It was still almost light – midsummer night – and there was a chill wind blowing in from the sea; this was the north coast of Aberdeenshire, after all. I had come to see butteries, also known as Aberdeen rowies, being made in the traditional way in a small bakery and it would surely be worth losing several hours' precious sleep.

Once he began his night's work, Alan McPherson reminded me of a juggler trying to keep all his balls in the air. After mixing a 'softie' dough, a brown bread dough, an oatmeal one and a pan bread, he finally began the butterie dough. The first stage had been prepared earlier – mixing some soft flour with white fat and lard. Despite the name, butter is never used because it makes them hard; they are called butteries because they are always eaten buttered. The bread dough was then mixed and kneaded with a large bread hook in one of the four mixers Alan was running around checking, filling and emptying. Then the dough was left to rest for half an hour before being folded neatly into a rectangle on the huge kneading table. By this stage there were five other doughs resting, all neatly tucked up and looking agonisingly like pillows. I, too, wanted to rest.

But I'd come to see the butterie from start to finish, so it was on to the next stage – folding and chopping the fat mixture into the bread dough. Then the mixture was cut into large rounds and each round into 30 pieces. Each of these was squashed into the classic butterie shape by hand on a baking sheet and left to rest again in a steam press or prover. It was now 2.30am, but once the rolls were baked in Alan's ancient Scotch oven (built between 1800 and 1830) I had to admit it had been worth staying up and being covered in fine clouds of flour for a taste of a warm butterie straight from the oven. Why eat croissants when you can have butteries?

Makes 16
450g/1lb strong white flour
20g/¾oz fresh yeast
20g/¾oz granulated sugar
about 300ml/10fl oz tepid water

For the fat dough:
250g/9oz white shortening
75g/3oz lard
20g/¾oz salt
50g/2oz plain flour

First prepare the fat dough by mixing all the ingredients together. Leave at room temperature so it is soft enough to work with.

Next make the bread dough. Place the flour in a bowl and make a well in the centre. Mix the yeast and sugar together, then mix into the water. Combine with the flour and knead by hand or with a dough hook until smooth; this will take about 10 minutes by hand. Place in a bowl, cover and leave for 30–45 minutes, until well risen. Then knock back the dough and roll it out into a long rectangle on a floured work surface.

Divide the fat dough into three and spread a third of it over the bread dough. Fold down the top third of the rectangle, then fold over again. Roll out to a rectangle once more and spread over another portion of fat dough. Fold and roll as before. Repeat this once more to use up the remaining fat dough. Then fold over. (Instead of rolling out the dough, Alan 'chops' the fat dough into it using a Scotch scraper, like a large spatula.) The dough should be slightly sticky and rough. Keep flouring your hands and the worksurface.

Cut the dough into 16 pieces and place these on a baking sheet. Shape them by pressing the front part of your floured hand – fingers only – on to each, so they are flattened and dimpled with fingerprints with one stroke. Then cover with a sheet of oiled clingfilm and leave to prove somewhere warm for 30 minutes. Preheat the oven to 220°C/425°F/Gas 7.

Bake the butteries for 25–30 minutes, until crisp and golden. Transfer to a wire rack to cool.

Ham and Haddie

Ham means bacon in Scotland and so this most comforting of breakfast dishes is quite simply smoked haddock (haddie) and bacon. It is traditionally made from finnan haddock (whole haddock with the head removed and the bone left in, then split – so the bone lies to one side – brined and cold-smoked), which is named after the village of Findon, south of Aberdeen, where the cure was perfected. For the ham, I suggest using dry-cure bacon but Parma ham is also excellent: grill or fry it for only a minute or two, until crisp.

This makes a delicious breakfast dish but is also good for tea. If you are serving it at teatime, a welcome addition is a little chopped parsley or lovage stirred into the cream sauce at the last minute.

Serves 1

1 finnan haddock

100ml/3½fl oz full-fat milk

40g/1½oz butter

2–3 rashers of dry-cure back bacon

2 tablespoons double cream

Place the finnan haddock in a saucepan with the milk and half the butter. Bring slowly to the boil, then cover and cook gently for 3–4 minutes until just done. Using 1 large or 2 medium spatulas, carefully transfer the fish to a serving plate and keep warm. Reserve the liquor in the pan.

Dry-fry or grill the bacon until crisp. Meanwhile, melt the remaining butter in another pan, stir in the cream and 2 tablespoons of the poaching liquid and let it bubble away for a minute or two until slightly thickened. Taste and add salt and pepper if necessary.

To serve, pour the sauce over the fish and top with the bacon. (A poached egg on top makes this wonderful breakfast dish sublime.)

Oatcakes

Although oatcakes are traditionally made on a girdle, I have given the oven method first, since most cooks are more familiar with baking trays than girdles. The classic way to make them is to cook one side on the girdle, then toast them on a special toasting stone in front of the fire. They are not turned over on the girdle to finish the cooking since this would make them tough. Once cool, the oatcakes are traditionally stored in a girnel (oatmeal chest) to keep them crisp. I bury mine in the large Tupperware box I keep porridge oats in.

The finished texture of the oatcakes will depend on the type of oatmeal you use: I like a base of medium oatmeal with either pinhead or fine added for a rough or smooth texture respectively. There are also regional variations on the thickness of the oatcake, from thin and crisp to thick and rough.

Oatcakes have long been part of the Scots' staple diet, with references to Scottish soldiers packing in their bag some oatmeal and a broad metal plate on which to cook oatcakes. It is recorded that Bonnie Prince Charlie's patriotic Highland soldiers set up roadside stalls to provide fresh oatmeal bannocks. The word bannock is interchangeable with oatcake in the west of Scotland, whereas in the east and north-east a bannock contains a proportion of wheat flour with the oatmeal to soften it. My recipe here is for crisp, not soft cakes.

Traditionally eaten for breakfast, oatcakes were also used to make sandwiches ('pieces') instead of bread. I can highly recommend them buttered, topped with a mature farmhouse Cheddar such as Isle of Mull or a blue cheese such as Lanark Blue or Dunsyre Blue, and sandwiched with another oatcake on top. This is messy but memorable picnic food.

Makes 8
175g/6oz medium oatmeal
50g/2oz fine or pinhead oatmeal
½ teaspoon salt
¼ teaspoon baking powder
25g/1oz butter, melted
about 50–75ml/2–3fl oz boiling water

Preheat the oven to 170°C/325°F/Gas 3. Place all the dry ingredients in a bowl and stir. Pour in the melted butter and enough boiling water to form a fairly stiff dough.

Sprinkle some fine or medium oatmeal over a board and gently roll out the mixture into a thin circle, about 23–25.5cm/9–10in diameter. Cut into 8 wedges and transfer carefully to a buttered baking tray. Bake in the oven for about 20 minutes, until just firm. Carefully transfer to a wire rack to cool.

Girdle method

Bake the oatcakes, 4 at a time, on a lightly buttered girdle over a moderate heat for 4–5 minutes on one side only. Once they are light brown underneath, transfer to a wire rack. Place this on a baking tray and set in a low oven (140°C/275°F/Gas 1) for about 25 minutes or until they have completely dried out. Leave to cool.

Barley Bannocks

There are many types of barley bannock but this recipe is from Shetland, where beremeal (barley flour) gruel or porridge is also eaten. These thick, hearty bannocks would be just the thing to warm you up – with a cup of tea or bowl of broth – before battling out against the bracing Shetland wind. The treacle is an optional extra but I like the rich colour and deep, sweet flavour it imparts.

As a general rule, a bannock is thicker and softer than an oatcake. Samuel Johnson wrote in his 1773 journal: 'Their native bread is made of oats or barley. Of oatmeal they spread very thin cakes, coarse and hard ... their barley cakes are thicker and softer: I began to eat them without unwillingness, the blackness of their colour raises some dislike but the taste is not disagreeable.'

Some bannocks, however, are as thin and pliable as chapatis, and indeed those I have seen in the Hebrides and Orkney (not Shetland) are thinnish and smaller – about 15cm/6in diameter. They are spread with butter then rolled up before being eaten.

Makes 4 thick bannocks
150g/5oz plain flour, sifted
200g/7oz barley flour (beremeal)
25g/1oz butter
1 dessertspoon black treacle
1 level teaspoon bicarbonate of soda
1½ teaspoons cream of tartar
250ml/9fl oz buttermilk or sour milk
(to sour milk, add 1 teaspoon lemon juice
and leave for 5 minutes)

Mix the flours together in a bowl and make a well in the centre. Melt the butter and treacle together and pour them into the well. Add the bicarbonate of soda and cream of tartar to the milk, stir well, then tip into the bowl. Combine everything gently but thoroughly. Using floured hands, turn out on to a lightly floured board and knead very gently to a thick round, about 25.5cm/10in diameter. Cut into quarters.

Heat a girdle over a medium heat, then grease very lightly, using a wad of kitchen paper. The heat should not be too high or the bannocks will burn before the insides are cooked. Place the bannocks on the girdle and leave for 4–5 minutes, until lightly coloured underneath, then turn. Leave for another 6–7 minutes, until cooked through. If necessary, tear the end off one to check that it is done inside. Transfer to a wire rack, then eat warm, split and spread with butter.

Baps

When I was a child, breakfast in bed, should I be so lucky, was a fried egg tucked neatly inside a soft, floury bap. This was impractical to eat in bed, as the minute you bit into it the yolk dripped down your chin and most probably on to the sheets. It was, however, sheer bliss.

Baps – or morning rolls as they are often called – are perfect for breakfast since they are soft, floury and unchallenging as the first food of the day. In Aberdeenshire they are called softies if they have no flour on them and floury baps if they do. Just as we picture every French household sending someone to fetch the morning baguette, so the Scottish family used to send a minion (usually the youngest member) to the baker's for morning rolls before breakfast on certain days – not every day, as porridge and toast were daily staples. Now most families have morning rolls on a Sunday, bought from the local newsagent with the Sunday papers. Split and spread with butter they are then eaten with bacon, egg, sausage or, my favourite, black pudding and tomato.

If you want to eat these freshly baked for breakfast, leave the dough in the fridge overnight for the first rising, then knock it back the next morning and continue with the recipe.

Makes 12
600g/1¼lb strong white flour,
plus extra for dusting
1 heaped teaspoon salt
7g packet of easy-blend/fast-action
dried yeast
25g/1oz butter, diced
about 350ml/12fl oz warm (hand-hot)
milk and water, mixed,
plus extra milk for brushing

Sift the flour and salt into a bowl and stir in the yeast. Rub in the butter, then make a well in the centre. Gradually pour in enough of the warm liquid to form a stiffish dough, bringing it together with lightly floured hands. Turn this out on to a lightly floured board and knead for about 10 minutes or until you feel it change from rough and nubbly to smooth and elastic. Place in a lightly oiled bowl and cover. Leave somewhere vaguely warm (I use my airing cupboard) for 1½–2 hours or until well risen.

Knock back the dough and divide into 12 pieces. Shape each into a round by rolling, then tucking any joins underneath so that the top is perfectly convex. Place well spaced apart on a lightly oiled baking sheet and cover loosely. Leave for about 30 minutes – again in a vaguely warm place.

Preheat the oven to 220°C/425°F/Gas 7. Using the heel of your hand, press down lightly on each bap to flatten it slightly. Brush the tops with milk and dust lightly with flour. Bake for about 15 minutes or until puffed up and golden brown. Eat warm.

Scrambled Eggs with Smoked Venison

Cold-smoked venison is not only good with eggs for breakfast. Try it as a starter with wedges of melon or figs, as you might serve Parma ham.

Be sure to serve these scrambled eggs shortly after stirring in the venison: you are not cooking the meat, just heating it through in the eggs. Accompany it with thick wholemeal toast.

Serves 1
3 medium free-range eggs
1 tbsp milk (or single or double cream)
25g /1oz butter
25g /1oz cold-smoked venison, slivered

Beat the eggs in a bowl with some salt and pepper and the milk or cream. Slowly melt the butter in a saucepan, then increase the heat to medium (not high) and add the egg mixture. Stirring frequently, cook for a maximum of 3-4 minutes, until it is just beginning to firm up. Remove from the heat, add the venison. Stir and serve at once.

Dundee Marmalade

This is fellow Dundonian and food writer Grace Mulligan's recipe for Seville marmalade, from her book, *Dundee Kitchen*. Grace recommends freezing Seville oranges during their short season in January and February. When using frozen fruit, you will need to add 2–3 extra oranges to the marmalade as the pectin content diminishes with freezing, reducing the ability to set.

The word marmalade comes from the Portuguese word for quinces, *marmelos*, and 'marmelada', a sugary, solid mass of quinces, was first mentioned in Britain's port records at the end of the fifteenth century. According to many accounts it was an enterprising young grocer, James Keiller, who first sold orange marmalade as we know it today, after his wife, Janet, used a consignment of bitter oranges (bought cheaply because they were inedible raw) to make it. This was apparently in the early 1700s, then by 1797 descendants of the Keillers opened their famous marmalade factory.

However, W. M. Mathew, in his book *Keiller's of Dundee*, declared this to be complete nonsense. The James who gave his name to the company was the son of Janet, not the husband, and he was only 22 and unmarried in 1797. What we know to be a fact, however, is that the Keillers were mainly confectioners, and did not specialise in marmalade until the 1800s, when they became the first firm to produce Scottish 'chip' marmalade. They did not invent the principles of marmalade making, as there was already a Scottish recipe for marmalade made from Seville sours in 1760 and an English recipe written by Sir Hugh Plat in 1605. James Boswell's wife Margaret sent home-made orange marmalade from Edinburgh to Samuel Johnson in London in 1777. What the Keillers did, however, was produce a specific and marketable product from Dundee, which soon became world famous.

The other fetching anecdote concerns Mary, Queen of Scots. As quinces were regarded at that time as a healing fruit, she took some with her on her voyage from France to Scotland in 1561. In order to alleviate her sea-sickness, the call was heard from her ladies, '*Marmalade pour Marie malade.*' Nice story, if you believe it!

Makes about 10 x 450g/1lb jars
1.3kg/3lb Seville oranges, scrubbed
2 lemons, scrubbed
3.5 litres/6 pints water
2.7kg/6lb granulated sugar
a knob of butter

Pour enough boiling water over the oranges and lemons to cover them. Leave until cool enough to handle, then cut the lemons in half and squeeze out the juice. Put the juice into a preserving pan or a large heavy-based pan and discard the skins. Cut the oranges in half and squeeze out most of the juice, then pour it into the pan. Put all the pips in a bowl. Cut each empty orange half into 3. Now, in 2 or 3 batches, place the orange peel in a food processor and process until it is chunky, watching to avoid overprocessing. Tip the chopped peel into the pan and add the water. Tie up the pips in a piece of muslin or fine nylon curtain and add to the pan. Cover and leave for about 6 hours or overnight to soften the peel.

Bring the contents of the pan to the boil, turn down the heat and simmer, uncovered, so the liquid will evaporate. Cook until it is a thick mush – this can take anything up to 2 hours – stirring often to prevent sticking.

Meanwhile, warm the sugar in a low oven. Add it to the fruit, stirring until dissolved, then turn up the heat and boil the marmalade for 15–20 minutes or until it reaches setting point (it may take longer). To test for setting point, put a teaspoon of marmalade on a cold saucer and refrigerate. After 1 minute, push the marmalade sideways; if it forms a skin the marmalade is ready. Lift the pan carefully on to a board and stir in the butter to disperse the foam. Pot the marmalade in warm sterilised jars (see below) and cover with a wax disc (or screw on metal lids). Cover with cellophane when cool (if using wax discs). Store in a cool, dark, dry place.

Note
To sterilise jam jars, wash them well in hot soapy water and then dry in a low oven. Alternatively, if you have a dishwasher you can put them through it and then microwave on I ligh for 1½ minutes.

Sassermaet

Sassermaet (sassermeat) is Shetland's sausagemeat – with a difference. Made primarily by butchers, it is still occasionally prepared at home and is basically raw salted beef mixed with fat, pepper, allspice, cinnamon, cloves and sometimes ginger or nutmeg. This is formed into a square or round mound and then sliced to order. It is fried (without fat, as it is fairly fatty) and served with either fried onion, egg or plain boiled potatoes. I like it with an egg fried in the fat from the pan. Delicious.

Serves 4
8 slices of sassermaet
1 large onion, peeled and sliced,
or 4 free-range eggs

Heat a dry frying pan and add the sassermaet. Cook for 2–3 minutes on each side, then remove from the pan and keep warm. Fry the onion or eggs in the fat and serve with the sassermaet.

Blackcurrant Jam

Apart from her famous raspberry jam, my mother made blackcurrant jam and jelly with fruit from our own blackcurrant bushes. She always employed my Great-Auntie Maggie's test for setting point: after boiling the jam for the requisite time, hold the wooden spoon high above the pan. Once most of the liquid has dropped off, run the nail of your forefinger along the back of the spoon. If it leaves a discernible line that is fairly solid, then it is ready.

Nowadays I go to my local pick-your-own farm with the children and pick strawberries and raspberries, but I buy the blackcurrants at the farm shop as the children don't enjoy eating them raw – and that is one of the greatest (illicit) pleasures of picking fruit straight from the field.

In Marion Lochhead's account of a Scots household in the eighteenth century, she writes, 'One of the noblest of conserves, blackcurrant jam, used to be kept as the most pleasant of remedies for colds and sore throats; a truly Scots touch.' A classic case of: it not only tastes good, it does you good, too!

Makes about 10 x 450g/1lb jars
1.8kg/4lb blackcurrants
1.75 litres/3 pints cold water
3kg/6½lb granulated sugar
a knob of butter (optional)

Place the blackcurrants in a preserving pan or a large deep saucepan with the water. Simmer gently for about 45 minutes, skimming off any scum from the surface, until the fruit is really soft. It is important that the skins are very soft before you add the sugar.

Add the sugar and stir until dissolved, then increase the heat. You can add the butter if you like, to help disperse the scum. Bring to the boil and boil rapidly for about 10 minutes or until setting point is reached. Test by my mother's method (above) or by dripping a little of the mixture on to a cold saucer: after a minute or two you should be able to run your forefinger through it, leaving a trail. Even when it is ready to pot, the mixture will look extremely runny. Don't panic; it will firm up nicely on cooling. This is not a stiff, solid jam, but rather a soft, spreadable one.

Pot immediately in warm sterilised jars (see page 19) and cover either at once or when completely cold. Label and store in a cool, dark, dry place.

Blackcurrant jam and butteries
(see page 10)

Raspberry Jam

This was the one jam my mother always had in stock because we had so many raspberries at the bottom of our garden. Her blackcurrant and apple jellies would often run out by early spring but raspberry lasted all year. I vividly remember the sweet, heady aromas of jam wafting out through the kitchen door, luring me into the house from playing in the garden in those long, halcyon days of childhood summers.

I like to add Drambuie to my raspberry jam to enhance the flavour. The recipe for this whisky-based liqueur was allegedly given by Bonnie Prince Charlie to Captain John MacKinnon, one of the Prince's most loyal Jacobite followers, in 1746. Many years later, in 1906, the MacKinnon descendants began its commercial production. I like to add splashes to any raspberry pudding and to many chocolate and ice-cream recipes.

Makes 3 x 450g/1lb jars
1kg/2¼lb fresh raspberries
1kg/2¼lb preserving sugar
(granulated will also do)
a knob of unsalted butter
1–2 tablespoons Drambuie (optional)

Place the raspberries in a preserving pan or a large, deep saucepan and simmer very gently for about 20 minutes, until they release their juices. Add the sugar and heat gently until dissolved, stirring constantly. Add the butter, then bring to the boil and boil rapidly for about 25 minutes or until setting point is reached. During this time, it will splatter – but don't be tempted to reduce the heat. I'm afraid you'll just have to wipe up after! Setting point is determined by placing a few drips of jam on a cold saucer and allowing it to cool quickly. Push it with your finger and if it wrinkles it is ready.

If using the Drambuie, add it now. Pot the jam in warm sterilised jars (see page 19) and seal either immediately or when completely cold. Label and store in a cool, dark, dry place.

Lemon Curd

I confess I always make my lemon curd in the microwave, as it is far quicker. This recipe is absolutely foolproof, presuming you follow the instructions and whisk or beat madly every minute; otherwise you will have sweet lemon scrambled eggs.

Although lemon curd cannot be claimed as as an exclusively Scottish recipe, it has been used extensively in Scotland for many years. I have seen versions made with heather honey instead of sugar, which might – or might not – add to its authenticity.

Use this at breakfast time to spread on toast, oatcakes or butteries. Since it is only worth preparing a decent-sized batch, use the rest to make luscious puddings (such as bread and butter pudding made with fruit loaf or Selkirk bannock), to fill rich, dark chocolate cake or to dollop on to pancakes or waffles.

Makes 3 x 450g/1lb jars
225g/8oz unsalted butter
450g/1lb granulated sugar
grated zest of 6 large unwaxed lemons
350ml/12fl oz freshly squeezed lemon juice
6 free-range eggs

Place the butter and sugar in a large, microwave-proof bowl with the lemon zest and juice. Cook, uncovered, on High, for 4–5 minutes, stirring every minute, until the butter has melted and the sugar dissolved. Remove and leave to cool for a couple of minutes.

Beat the eggs together and strain them through a sieve. Whisk them into the bowl, then return it to the microwave. Cook for 6–8 minutes, removing and whisking madly every minute.

When the curd has thickened to the consistency of lightly whipped cream (it will firm up more on cooling) pour it at once into warm sterilised jars (see page 19). Tap to level the surface and remove any air bubbles, then wipe the jars. Label and seal only when completely cold. Store in the refrigerator for up to 6 weeks.

2

soups

Soup is something we do well in Scotland. Always have done. Since the first kail-pot was hung over a peat fire, we have chopped and stirred, simmered and supped. Local produce – mutton, lamb or beef bones, barley, root vegetables and kail – have been thrown into the pot with water and cooked to nourishing perfection.

Well-known soups such as Scotch broth, cock-a-leekie and Cullen skink need little preface. But allow me to introduce you to crab- and rice-based partan bree, Shetland's memorable reestit (reested) mutton soup and my great-grandmother's magnificent hare soup, known in Scotland as bawd bree. All these can be meals in themselves, served in large bowls with bread, bannocks or oatcakes on the side. Or they can be served in shallow soup plates as a starter, which is how I ate soup every day as a child, come rain, hail or shine. Yes, even in the heatwaves of nostalgic childhood summers, there was always hot soup to come home to. It was part of growing up in Scotland.

And when we were ill, a mug of soup was always first on the invalid's menu. It is surely no coincidence that when we are unwell or just a little under the weather, our bodies crave soup. Hearty vegetable soup, wholesome lentil soup or perhaps a light chicken broth – they all slip down gently while nourishing the body and soothing the soul. In my opinion you can forget bangers and mash or jam roly-poly in the comfort-food stakes. Give me a good bowl of soup any day (with steamed treacle pudding and custard afterwards . . . assuming my infliction was not life-threatening).

Some references suggest that the Scots' soup-making skills should be attributed to the French and the Auld Alliance. Whereas certain soups and pottages seem to be directly linked, it is a fact that long before the claret trade began with Leith and before Mary, Queen of Scots sailed from France to reside in Edinburgh, we were ladling out delicious soups. They were undoubtedly not grand, complicated or sophisticated but rather homely, hearty and nourishing. Which is my idea of perfection in a soup bowl, whether I am feeling well or – as we say in Scotland – awfy no' weel.

Kail Brose

Many broths made with oatmeal are known as brose. This one is typical of several regions of Scotland, where kail or curly kale used to be widely grown throughout the winter; the vegetable suits the Scottish climate admirably because of its ability to withstand frost. It also provided an essential intake of vitamins and minerals throughout the cold, bleak winter months. The kail-yard was the common term for the kitchen garden, where vegetables were grown. So essential was this hardy vegetable to the diet that in parts of Lowland and north-east Scotland, kail was also the name given to the midday meal. The iron kail-pot and iron girdle were the two most basic pieces of cooking equipment found in crofts and cottages. Besides being made into broths and soups, it was also served on its own, with butter and milk added when available. Dr Samuel Johnson remarked in his *Journey to the Western Islands of Scotland* that 'when they [the Scots] had not kail, they probably had nothing'.

Ena Baxter in her *Scottish Cookbook* describes kail brose as one of her least favourite childhood meals. The way it was eaten was similar to the porridge ritual, with milk and porridge in separate bowls. She describes how oatmeal was placed in each bowl with a pinch of salt, then a ladleful of boiling hot beef broth stirred in and the puréed kail served separately. A spoonful of kail was dipped into the broth and the two eaten together, swilled down with a glass of milk. At the onset of spring, nettles would often be substituted for kail but in this case a lighter chicken stock was likely to be used to suit the more delicate flavour of nettles.

Instead of using ready-made stock, it is more authentic to boil up a piece of ox head, cow heel or marrowbone with water first to make some good fatty stock, which is best for this recipe. So if you get your hands on a heel or a head, boil away!

Serves 4
300g/10½oz kail (curly kale),
well washed, stalks removed
1.2 litres/2 pints hot beef stock
50g/2oz medium oatmeal
1 heaped teaspoon salt
thick oatcakes and butter, to serve

Place the kail in a large saucepan with the hot stock and bring to the boil. Then cook, uncovered, over a medium heat for 10–15 minutes, until tender. Meanwhile, place the oatmeal on a sheet of foil and toast under a hot grill for 3–4 minutes, until golden brown, shaking often so it does not burn.

Using a slotted spoon, transfer the kail to a blender and purée with a ladle or so of the stock, then return it to the pan. Add the salt and plenty of freshly milled pepper. Gradually add most of the toasted oatmeal and, stirring constantly to avoid lumps, cook for 4–5 minutes, until thickened. Check the seasoning and ladle the soup into warmed bowls. Sprinkle over the remaining oatmeal and serve with buttered oatcakes.

Partan Bree

This is a rich, creamy crab soup: partan means crab, bree is liquid or gravy. If you are using a live crab as your base, boil it for 15–20 minutes, then remove the creamy brown body meat and place in a bowl; put the sweet white (claw and leg) meat in another. Discard the feathery 'dead men's fingers' as you work. You can buy cooked crab from a fishmonger but avoid dressed ones, as these sometimes have other ingredients added to them such as breadcrumbs.

Popular in many seaside areas of Scotland, this recipe has, of course, variations. Lady Clark of Tillypronie suggested adding some anchovy (presumably anchovy essence); I also rather like a shake or two of Worcestershire sauce. I have included a blade of mace for extra flavour.

Serves 4–6
75g/3oz long-grain rice
600ml/1 pint full-fat milk
a blade of mace
the meat of 1 large crab or about
300g/10½oz fresh or defrosted frozen
crabmeat (about 200g/7oz brown meat
and 100g/3½oz white meat)
600ml/1 pint hot fish stock
150ml/5fl oz double cream (optional)
anchovy essence

Put the rice, milk and mace in a pan, bring to the boil and simmer for about 15–20 minutes, until the rice is tender. Discard the mace and tip the rice and milk into a liquidiser or food processor with the brown crabmeat. Process until combined, then pour back into the pan and add the hot stock. Place over a medium heat until just below boiling point, then add the white crabmeat and the cream, if using. Heat gently for a couple of minutes, then add salt, pepper and anchovy essence to taste. Serve in warm bowls and add an extra dash of anchovy essence – and extra cream – to each portion if you like.

Arbroath Fishermen's Soup

My brother-in-law Jim's friend, Alec Smith, has been a fisherman in Arbroath for over a quarter of a century. He goes to sea in the family boat to catch mainly haddock and whiting. During the four or five days they are at sea, there is plenty of fish on board. And so this old family recipe comes into its own. The soup is prepared one day, then reheated the next. The quantities are large but it is more main meal than first course. Once it has fed the entire crew – or just your family – it will keep in the fridge for a couple of days.

The addition of evaporated milk might seem rather bizarre but that is what the fishermen take to sea instead of fresh milk to put in their tea. If you do not approve, use double cream instead.

Serves 10

2 large onions, peeled and chopped

6 medium potatoes, peeled and cut into large chunks

2 heaped tablespoons medium oatmeal

1 level tablespoon salt

6 thick haddock fillets (about 1.5kg/3lb 5oz in total), each cut into about 8 large chunks

300ml/10fl oz evaporated milk, or 150ml/5fl oz double cream

chopped parsley and thick oatcakes, to serve

Place the onions, potatoes and oatmeal in a very large saucepan with 2.25 litres/4 pints of cold water. Add the salt and plenty of freshly ground pepper. Bring to the boil, skimming off any scum. Once it is bubbling, add the fish, then cover the pan and reduce the heat to a simmer. Cook for 10 minutes, just until the potatoes are tender. (If you are cooking it the day before, as the fishermen do, remove from the heat at this stage and leave to cool completely before refrigerating or keeping somewhere cold. The next day, reheat gently until piping hot.) Stir in the evaporated milk or cream and check the seasoning. Ladle into warmed bowls, sprinkle over some parsley, crumble over some oatcakes and serve at once.

Cullen Skink

There are many different recipes for Cullen skink. The one I ate at the Seaforth Hotel in Cullen, made by chef Gareth Eddy, was flavoured with leeks, thyme, mustard and even garlic – delicious, although not exactly traditional. The classic one is made with whole finnan haddock (finnan haddie) but you can use smoked haddock fillets instead – make sure they are undyed. Jerusalem artichokes are also wonderful in this soup instead of potatoes.

Serves 6

2 finnan haddock or 500g/18oz undyed smoked haddock fillets

2 onions, peeled and finely chopped

2 large potatoes (about 600g/1¼lb), peeled and finely diced

450ml/16fl oz full-fat milk

25g/1oz unsalted butter

double cream and chopped chives, to garnish

Put the haddock in a large pan with 300ml/10fl oz cold water. Bring to the boil and simmer for 5–10 minutes, until the fish is just cooked (finnan haddock will need a little longer than fillets). Remove the fish with a slotted spoon and flake into large chunks (discard the bones if using finnan haddock), then set aside.

Add the onions and potatoes to the pan with plenty of pepper. Pour in some of the milk if the water doesn't cover the vegetables, then cover the pan and cook over a moderate heat for 12–15 minutes, until tender. Remove the pan from the heat and, using a potato masher, roughly mash the contents, keeping some of the texture. Add the milk and butter and bring to the boil, then simmer for a couple of minutes. Add the fish and reheat gently for 2–3 minutes. Season to taste, then serve in warm bowls with a swirl of cream and some chopped chives.

Cock-a-Leekie

This is hailed by many to be Scotland's other national soup, and it never ceases to amaze me how such a delicious soup can be made from so few ingredients. I like to serve the broth in bowls and the chicken on a separate ashet (platter) to be carved at table, then the pieces dropped into the soup as required. Alternatively, the cook can chop the meat in the kitchen and reheat it in the soup just before serving. The main thing is to avoid overcooking the chicken, otherwise it will be tough. Traditional recipes recommend simmering it for 4 hours (in those days, an old boiling fowl would probably have been used), then serving at once. I like to cook the chicken only for 20 minutes or so, leave it to cool in the stock, then reheat the bird either whole or in pieces. I also discard the rather slimy green part of the leeks and replace them with the white part, which is cooked until just done.

In Scott's *The Fortunes of Nigel*, the king (James VI and I) says, 'My lords and lieges, let us all to dinner for the cockie-leekie is a-coolin' – which reminds us that this is a very old dish. Interestingly some recipes exclude the prunes, but I think they are essential for their contrasting sweetness.

Serves 6
1 free-range chicken, weighing about
1.1–1.3kg/2½–3lb
6 long, thick leeks (choose ones with
plenty of green and white)
10–12 black peppercorns
12–16 stoned prunes
1 tablespoon chopped parsley

Place the chicken in a large saucepan. Halve the leeks lengthways, wash them well, then cut off the green parts. Chop these roughly and add to the pan with the peppercorns and enough water just to cover: about 2 litres/3½ pints. Bring slowly to the boil, then cover and simmer for about 20 minutes. Remove from the heat, cover tightly and leave for about an hour.

Then take out the chicken and use a slotted spoon to remove the leeks, which can be discarded. Chop the white part of the leeks, add to the pan with the prunes and bring to the boil again. Simmer for about 10 minutes, until the leeks are just done.

If you are serving the chicken whole, return it to the pan for the last 3–5 minutes or so to warm through. Otherwise, remove the chicken flesh from the bones, chop it into pieces and add these to the soup. Add plenty of salt and pepper to taste and serve with the chopped parsley on top.

Tattie Soup

Although this is traditionally made with mutton stock, my recipe uses chicken stock, which I reckon more people are likely to have at home. It must be good quality, however, preferably from a free-range or organic chicken.

If you make this in late spring or early summer, you could add a handful of chopped young nettle leaves a couple of minutes before serving.

Serves 6–8
1.2 litres/2 pints good chicken stock
(I use about 850ml/1½ pints jellied stock
mixed with 300ml/10fl oz water.)
1kg/2¼lb potatoes, peeled and diced
1 large onion, peeled and diced
3–4 carrots, peeled and diced
chopped chives, parsley or young
nettle leaves

Bring the stock to the boil in a large saucepan. Add the vegetables and some salt and pepper, then cover and cook over a medium heat for 25–30 minutes, until all the vegetables are tender. Taste and check the seasoning.

If using nettle leaves, stir them in and heat through for 2 minutes. If using chives or parsley, sprinkle each portion with some after ladling the soup into bowls.

Dulse Soup

Margaret Horn is a highly respected Scottish cook who has not wandered far from her roots. Born and brought up in Auchmithie, a tiny village nestling on the cliffs three miles north of Arbroath, she and her husband have owned The But 'n' Ben since 1977. Because seaweed was part of her childhood diet, she has incorporated it into some dishes served at the restaurant. Dulse and tangles (kelp) are two of her favourite seaweeds and not only does she cook with them, she also nibbles on them as she picks the seaweed whenever the tide is out. She uses tangles (*Laminaria digitata*) to wrap up haddock for steaming. The dulse (*Palmaria (Rhodymenia) palmata*) is made into a simple soup, particularly in the winter months when it is tougher and less suitable for grilling. It is surprising how flavoursome this soup is, for no stock is used, but the pure flavour of the sea comes through in a pleasingly distinctive yet not overpowering way.

When picking wild seaweed, ensure it is from clean water and that there is not a sewage plant lurking just around the bay! Dried dulse can be substituted for fresh. For this recipe use a minimum of 50g/2oz dried dulse and soak it in water for 5–10 minutes first.

Serves 6
about 200g/7oz freshly picked dulse,
well washed
4 large potatoes, peeled and chopped
2 onions, peeled and chopped

Place all the ingredients in a large saucepan and add enough water to cover. Bring to the boil, then simmer for about 10 minutes or until the potatoes are tender. Purèe in a blender, then reheat gently, adding salt and pepper to taste. Serve as it is or garnished with some grilled dulse (see page 110).

Reested Mutton Soup

It was at the opening of Edinburgh's latest restaurant, Restaurant Martin Wishart – which has become one the city's best – that I met Georgia Wishart, Martin's mother. She and I talked, not of the foie gras millefeuille nor the heavenly chocolate délice on our plates, but of reested mutton, brunnies and krappin. For Georgia was born and brought up in a remote part of Shetland, the westerly hamlet of Garderhouse. As a child she ate porridge (oatmeal or beremeal), boiled 'piltak' (two-year-old saithe), which her father would catch with a fishing line from the rowing boat he built himself, brunnies (wholemeal girdle scones), beremeal bannocks and tattie soup flavoured with reested mutton. Some weeks later, Georgia cooked her soup for me and I was charmed by its flavour.

Reested (reestit) mutton is cured mutton that has been salted for at least 10 days, then hung up on hooks to dry (preferably over a peat fire) for as long as it takes to be eaten up. After some time it looks rather like salt cod, with an ivory hue and a stiff, cardboard feel. Some people have it hanging there for so long that they wrap newspapers around it to prevent the dust settling. The mutton is then sliced as thinly as Parma ham and fried with onions, or, best of all, made into soup. Georgia's soup had both the smell and taste of mutton and was thick and chunky with vegetables. After just one bowl of it, I was hooked – the flavour is so distinctive. It is well worth the long trek north to Shetland any day.

Reested mutton was traditionally eaten during the winter months, when there was little fresh meat available, and it can still be found in butcher's shops in the run-up to Christmas.

Serves 6–8
450g/1lb reested mutton
1 onion
4–5 large carrots
1 medium turnip (called swede in England)
6–8 floury potatoes

Place the mutton in a large pan and cover with cold water. Bring to the boil and simmer for about 30 minutes. Peel all the vegetables and chop them into good-size chunks, then add them to the soup. Return to the boil and cook, covered, until everything is tender – about 20 minutes. Remove the meat from the pan, cut off slices and put them on a plate. Serve the soup piping hot, with the plate of sliced meat on the side.

Scotch Broth

'This is the comfortable *pot au feu* of Scotland,' wrote Meg Dods about Scotland's national soup. Most people enjoying a bowl of broth as a starter might not see the similarities but, served (as it was and often still is) in two parts – as a soup course, then with the meat and freshly boiled vegetables to follow – it is closer to France's famous *pot au feu* than any other dish. Often tiny whole potatoes, turnips or carrots would be added with the other vegetables and cooked until tender, then removed to an ashet (platter) and arranged around the meat.

As I grew up, there was always a pot of soup sitting on the cooker, whatever the weather, and broth was the favourite. When my mother and father were children in Dundee, there was broth to start every dinnertime. Like so many things that were good for you, it was seldom talked about, just eaten, but what a health-giving soup it is, packed full of freshly cooked vegetables and meat stock. Meg Dods also described it as 'the bland, balsamic barley-broth of Scotland'. And whereas bland I would disagree with, the word balsamic (before its connotations of fashionable vinegars arose) describes it aptly. For after a plate of broth, all seems well with the world. It is soothing and comforting, invigorating and restorative. It is the Scots' panacea, our very own Jewish chicken soup. The critical Dr Samuel Johnson, however, ate several platefuls of broth, and had his own opinion. 'You never ate it before?' inquired James Boswell, his travelling companion in their 1773 tour of the Highlands. 'No sir, but I don't care how soon I eat it again.'

Finally, I should warn you that my recipe might produce a soup that is too thick and hearty for some people's tastes. If that is the case, simply add more boiling water after the initial cooking. Bear in mind that my idea of good broth is summed up in the opening lines of Robert Crawford's poem 'Scotch Broth': 'A soup so thick you could shake its hand and stroll with it before dinner.'

Serves 6
a piece of boiling beef
(runner, thin rib or flank), or
neck of mutton or shoulder of lamb,
weighing about 700g/1½lb
150g/5oz dried marrowfat peas,
soaked overnight and then drained
75g/3oz pearl barley,
soaked overnight and then drained
25g/1oz parsley (including the stalks)
200g/7oz carrots, peeled and finely diced
150g/5oz kail (curly kale),
washed and finely chopped
200g/7oz turnip (called swede in England),
peeled and finely diced
1 large onion, peeled and finely chopped

Place the meat in a large pan with the soaked peas and barley and the parsley stalks. Cover with cold water – about 2.25 litres/4 pints – and bring slowly to the boil. Then skim off any scum and reduce to a simmer. Cover and cook for at least 1 hour or until the peas are tender. Remove the parsley stalks if possible (don't worry if some remain) and add all the vegetables. Bring to the boil again and cook for about 20 minutes, until the vegetables are tender. Chop the parsley and add most of it to the soup, with salt and pepper to taste.

To serve, remove the meat from the pan and cut it into pieces. Add these to the soup and serve sprinkled with the remaining parsley. You could, if you like, serve the vegetable broth first, then the beef as a main course, in which case add a few tiny whole vegetables with the diced ones to serve with the meat.

Mussel Brose

This is a delicious soup for a bitterly cold winter's day. The mussels are cooked lightly, then their liquor reheated with some milk and fish stock and thickened with oatmeal – hence the name brose. The mussels are returned to the pan towards the end and it is served in warm bowls with a scattering of chives. Perhaps the etymology of brose goes back to the Ancient Greek and Latin ambrosia – food of the gods.

Serves 4
1kg/2¼lb mussels
300ml/10fl oz milk
300ml/10fl oz fish stock
75g/3oz fine oatmeal, toasted
chopped chives, to garnish
a little cream, to serve (optional)

Scrub the mussels thoroughly, discarding any open ones that don't close when tapped on a work surface. Place in a pan with 600ml/1 pint of cold water. Cover tightly and bring slowly to the boil, shaking the pan a couple of times. Boil for about 1 minute or until the mussels have opened, then remove from the heat and strain over a large jug.

Heat together the milk, fish stock and 600ml/1 pint of the mussel liquor. Bring slowly to the boil, then reduce the heat to medium. Put the oatmeal in a bowl. Remove a ladleful of the liquid from the pan and add it to the oatmeal, stirring until smooth. Add this mixture gradually to the pan, whisking or stirring well until smooth (if it is still rather 'knotty', tip into a blender and whiz until smooth). Cook gently for a couple of minutes.

Remove the mussels from their shells and return them to the pan. Reheat gently for a minute or so, then season to taste. Serve in warm bowls with some chopped chives and a swirl of cream, if you like.

Hare Soup

Every year my father and his brother and sisters used to go to their grandmother's home in Dundee for the family Christmas meal, hare soup (bawd bree in Scots). Since she had been in service in one of the big estates in Angus, my great-grandmother was an expert in dealing with game. My aunts can still remember the tiny chunks of hare throughout the soup and its rich, gamy taste. My father simply remembers that it was not his favourite; that's because it was not mince and tatties.

A dollop of cranberry sauce or redcurrant jelly stirred into the soup just before serving is by no means authentic but it does contrast beautifully with the rich flavour.

Serves 6

1 hare, skinned, cleaned and cut into pieces

40g/1½oz flour, seasoned with salt and pepper

60g/2½oz butter

2 large onions, peeled and chopped

75g/3oz unsmoked streaky bacon, chopped

3–4 carrots, peeled and chopped

2 celery sticks, chopped

2–3 sprigs of parsley

2–3 sprigs of thyme

1.5 litres/2½ pints hot beef stock

50ml/2fl oz port

My butcher advises washing the hare pieces in salt before cooking: just put them in the sink and rub with salt, then rinse under cold running water before patting thoroughly dry.

Dip the hare in the seasoned flour and brown all over in 40g/1½oz of the butter in a large heavy pan (you will need to do this in batches). Remove the meat from the pan. Add the remaining butter and gently fry the onions and bacon in it for about 10 minutes. Add the carrots and celery and cook for about 5 minutes, then return the meat to the pan with the herbs, hot stock and some salt and pepper. Bring to the boil, skim if necessary, then cover and simmer gently for about 2 hours (an older, tougher hare will need about 3 hours).

Remove the hare pieces from the pan and leave until cool enough to handle, then tear the meat into small pieces. Purée the soup in a blender and return it to the pan with the meat. Stir in the port, reheat gently, then add salt and pepper to taste. Once it is hot, check if it needs any extra port – a final splash would not go amiss.

3

fresh and smoked fish

Turn the clock back a couple of decades and take a look in a
Scottish fishmonger's window. There would be little other than
haddock, sole and herring. And some of the haddock was totally
unrecognisable, dressed as it was in a hideous orange robe called
ruskoline. Fast-forward to the present day and there is an increasing
interest in fish, resulting in fishmonger's slabs covered with snapper,
tuna, orange roughy and hoki, mostly air-freighted in from the other
side of the world. All well and good, we must expand our palate, but
not to the detriment of our own produce.

There has been an increasing interest in fish from our own
shores, too, although a slightly unfortunate result of this is the
establishment of so many salmon farms, which have not always
proved beneficial to either the environment or the fish industry.
Fishmongers are happy to offer alternatives to traditional fish, say,
ling instead of haddock for fish pie, or mackerel instead of herring to
be fried in oatmeal for tea. And with more piscine awareness from
customers, there is a general feeling that fish is *the* food for the
turn of the century, as it is light, versatile and exceedingly healthy.

Although, sadly, the reduction of cod and haddock quotas because
of over-fishing means that fishmongers and chip shops might have
to alter their range, there are still other fish in the sea. And, of
course, in our rivers.Cured fish, particularly smoked fish, have been
an important part of Scotland's heritage for centuries. Arbroath
smokies, finnan haddock and oak-smoked salmon are well known
worldwide and are now more easily available in good fishmonger's
and by mail order.

Some of the fish dishes in this chapter are classics – herring in
oatmeal, Tweed kettle and potted salmon, for example. But others
may baffle you with their intriguing titles. Crappit heid, hairy tatties
and cabbie-claw might not be the first thing you think of for a
simple Friday fish supper *à deux* but do give them a try. Like
so many old Scottish recipes, they may not win prizes for their
looks but, my, how they taste good.

Tatties and Herring

This is a ridiculously simple dish but tastes absolutely delicious when made with good salt herring. One of the oldest references to curing herring is in Martin Martin's book on the Western Islands, written in 1703. In his day, herrings were cured by hanging them up in the smoky rafters to dry. But in spite of prohibitive salt duties, pickling or salting the herring in barrels soon took over from air-drying and eventually became the customary method of preserving them. By the mid-nineteenth century, salted herring formed a crucial part of the crofters' winter diet in the Western Isles.

In Ena Baxter's *Scottish Cookbook*, she writes that the herring industry became established around the Caithness coast in the 1790s, which meant that during the nineteenth century, tatties and herring was the staple diet of most Caithness people. Until relatively recently, most Caithness cottages had a 'firkin' (a small wooden barrel for salting fish) at their door to last them throughout the winter. The herrings were packed in these barrels over layers of salt, head to tail alternately.

In *Growing Up in Scotland*, there are some lovely recollections from an Aberdeenshire man from 1910: 'My brother would collect fish that had dropped while they were unloading the boats and loading up the carts. He would put one on each finger through the gills to carry them. He went round the doors with them and got tuppence a dozen for his herrin' and that was all profit since he hadn't had to pay for them. Everybody had a barrel of salt herrin' for the winter.'

The usual way to eat salt herring is to soak them in water (milk in Shetland) and either boil the herring and potatoes separately (as they do in the Hebrides) or layer them in a pot and cook them together. Whichever way you choose, it is important to use unpeeled potatoes. And it is customary to eat the herrings with your fingers, to tackle the bones more easily.

I buy salt herring from my fishmonger but if yours does not sell them they are easy to prepare yourself. My fishmonger removes the gills and gently pulls out the long gut, leaving the head.

(The fish is not slit for normal gutting as the 'melts' – soft roe – are left in.) They are then cleaned and packed in dry salt for about six weeks. Traditionally they are eaten on Hogmanay (Auld Year's Night) because they cleanse the body after Christmas excess. They also arouse a great thirst . . .

Serves 6
6 salt herring
12–18 potatoes, scrubbed

First soak the salt herring for 24 hours, changing the water a couple of times.

Method 1
Fill a heavy-based pot with scrubbed unpeeled potatoes and add enough water to come half way up the potatoes. Rinse the soaked herring and place them on top. Cover tightly, bring to the boil and simmer until the potatoes are tender.

Method 2
I prefer this method, as the fish cannot overcook and more salt is removed. Place the soaked herring in a pan of cold water, bring to the boil and then carefully tip out the water. Refill with cold water and bring to the boil again. Remove from the heat, cover and allow to cool, by which time the herrings will be cooked. Meanwhile, boil the potatoes in their jackets in another pan.

To serve, dish the fish and potatoes out on to each plate straight from the pan. Milk is the traditional drink.

Salmon with Lemon Thyme Butter

In Mistress Dods' *Cook and Housewife's Manual of 1829*, her instructions for baking salmon or trout include a sprig of lemon thyme in the vinegar mixture to pickle the fish once cooked. I have developed this idea to make a lemon thyme butter for serving with simply seared salmon. Boiled new potatoes and a green vegetable are good with this dish.

Serves 4

4 middle-cut salmon fillets,
weighing about 200g/7oz each,
pin-bones removed, skinned

olive oil

For the lemon thyme butter:
75g/3oz unsalted butter, softened
2 heaped tablespoons finely chopped
lemon thyme leaves

To make the lemon thyme butter, beat the butter until smooth, then beat in the thyme and some salt and pepper. Spoon on to a sheet of foil and mould into a sausage shape, then roll up in the foil and chill until solid.

Put the salmon on a plate, rub all over with olive oil and set aside for 30 minutes. Heat a heavy-based frying pan or griddle pan until very hot – this can take up to 10 minutes. Smear the base with oil, using a wad of kitchen paper, then, once it is very hot again, add the salmon. Season with salt and pepper and turn after 2 minutes, by which time a good crust should have formed. Continue cooking until just done – 2–4 minutes depending on thickness.

Cut off discs of the lemon thyme butter. Serve the fish on warm plates with a couple of discs of butter on top.

Potted Salmon

This is ideal to make after you have cooked Tweed Kettle (see page 47) or whenever you have some cooked salmon left over. Serve with lemon wedges and brown toast or oatcakes.

Serves 6–8

400g/14oz cooked salmon, in chunks
100g/3½oz unsalted butter, softened
6 anchovy fillets, snipped
scant ¼ teaspoon ground mace
a good pinch of cayenne pepper

Put all the ingredients in a bowl and pound together with a wooden spoon until combined. Alternatively process in a food processor, using the pulse button – it should have some texture, rather than being a homogeneous paste. Season to taste with salt and pepper and pile into small dishes. Chill well before eating, spread thickly on toast or oatcakes.

Cabbie-Claw

I'll admit that I was not keen on the idea of this dish initially – salted cod with a parsley and egg sauce. But then I remembered the divine brandade of Provence, which is basically salt cod beaten with milk and oil, and the delicious Caribbean saltfish cakes made with salt cod and potatoes. My Scottish recipe had parsley, horseradish and cayenne to zap it up, so it was definitely worth a go.

In Shetland the dialect word for codling is kabbilow, which is very similar to the name of this dish. However, some historians believe the possible etymological link is from the French for cod, *cabillaud*. But perhaps a more likely theory – because of all the trade between Scotland and Holland – is that it derives from the Dutch for cod, *kabeljauw*.

Cabbie-claw is a very old dish, dating back to the times when preserving fish did not mean slinging it in a freezer. Instead it was salted, wind-dried, then stored for use throughout the year, usually to be cooked and served with mashed potatoes. The introduction of an egg and parsley sauce was obviously a later, more sophisticated idea, and I include it here because it does enhance the dish. Which, incidentally, despite my misgivings, I found absolutely delicious.

You could also serve the salted cod without the egg sauce, dunked into a caper-heavy salsa verde – inauthentic but surprisingly good.

Serves 6
1 very fresh young codling, weighing about 1.1kg/2½lb
salt (my fishmonger uses fine powdered salt; I recommend regular table salt)
a handful of parsley stalks (use the leaves for the sauce)
1 tablespoon horseradish sauce

For the egg sauce:
40g/1½oz butter
40g/1½oz plain flour
200ml/7fl oz milk
3 large free-range eggs, hard-boiled and chopped
a handful of chopped parsley leaves
cayenne pepper

Ask your fishmonger to remove the head of the fish, leaving the lugs on (the lugs are the hard bones connecting the head to the undergill). The guts should then be removed and the fish should be thoroughly cleaned by scrubbing. Then it should be split on one side, so that the bone remains to one side, leaving a flat fish. Wipe well.

Sprinkle a good 1cm/½in layer of salt into a large plastic or china container, then place the fish on top. Cover it with another thick layer of salt. Cover and leave somewhere cool (a larder, not a fridge) for 24 hours. The next day, the fish will be sitting in a puddle of thick brine. Remove it and hang it up to dry. To do this, insert a knitting needle or a skewer through the lugs and hang it up with a hook (I hang it from a large pair of steps or an upturned stool and place a bowl underneath for excess brine to drip into). Ideally it should be placed somewhere cool and breezy, preferably in the fresh air in a strong wind. But unless you want all the neighbourhood cats around, just place it somewhere draughty with cool air circulating. Leave for 24–36 hours, depending on the outside temperature, then rinse thoroughly under a running tap, removing all salt adhering to the outsides.

Place the fish in a large saucepan of cold water. Bring slowly to the boil, then, when you see bubbles, pour away all the water. Cover again with cold water, add the parsley stalks and the horseradish and bring slowly to the boil. Do not actually allow it to boil: this makes it hard. Cover, and simmer gently for 15 minutes, then carefully lift the fish out and drain the liquid into a jug. Once the fish is cool, remove the skin and bones, break the flesh into large chunks and place in a dish. Keep warm while you make the sauce.

Melt the butter in a pan, stir in the flour and cook for a minute or two, then gradually add 300ml/10fl oz of the hot fish cooking liquid and the milk, whisking until smooth. Simmer for 10–15 minutes, then taste and add pepper if necessary – no salt. Stir in the chopped eggs and parsley and pour the sauce over the fish. Dust lightly with cayenne pepper to serve.

Tweed Kettle

Basically a poached salmon dish (originally using fish from the River Tweed), Tweed kettle is extremely versatile as it can be served warm or cold, or used to make Potted Salmon (see page 44). When poaching salmon, it is essential never to add salt to the poaching liquid, as this can stiffen the flesh of the fish.

Serves 8
A large bunch of dill
12 black peppercorns
3 fresh bay leaves
1.8kg/4lb tail-end piece of salmon, cleaned
300ml/10fl oz white wine

Place the dill, peppercorns and bay leaves along the rack of a fish kettle. Put the fish on top and pour over the wine, then pour over enough cold water just to cover the fish. Bring slowly to the boil; this will take a good 15–20 minutes. Once the liquid is boiling, allow to bubble for 3 minutes, then switch off the heat, cover tightly with the lid and leave until completely cold, which can take up to 4 hours. If you want to serve the salmon warm, remove after 3 hours.

Lift out the rack, shake dry, place a serving dish on top and invert: the uppermost side of the salmon should now have a dill and peppercorn pattern. Serve with new potatoes, green vegetables and mayonnaise.

Potted Herring

Potted (or soused) herring is a typical teatime dish, eaten with salad and potatoes or brown bread and butter. Lady Clark of Tillypronie recommends serving it for breakfast and also suggests cooking sea trout in the same way.

My fishmonger advises using smaller herring to make this, as they are the sweetest and so no sugar is required in the sousing. Also, the vinegar and water solution will dissolve the tiny featherbones easily in small fish; larger ones have harder bones, which take longer to dissolve.

I have occasionally wrapped the herring in sheets of nori (dried Japanese seaweed) for a change, but you must skin the herring before wrapping. If using nori, smear a little wasabi (Japanese horseradish) over the fillets first.

Serves 4–6

6–8 boned herring (about 75–100g/3–3½oz each, after boning)

1 medium onion, peeled and sliced

150ml/5fl oz white wine vinegar

150ml/5fl oz water

10–12 black peppercorns

a blade of mace

2 fresh bay leaves

Preheat the oven to 180°C/350°F/Gas 4. Season the herring inside with salt and pepper. Scatter half the onion slices over the base of an ovenproof dish. Roll up the herring from the tail end, with the skin side out, and place them on top of the onion, packing them tightly together to keep them rolled up. (Don't worry that the fins are still on –they will come away easily once cooked. Trying to remove them before cooking will only result in a large hole in the back.) Scatter over the remaining onion slices.

Put the vinegar, water, peppercorns, mace and bay leaves in a saucepan, bring to the boil, then pour it over the herring: the liquid should almost cover the fish. Cover tightly and bake in the oven for 25 minutes, then remove and leave, still covered, until cold.

Herring (or Trout) in Oatmeal

Another traditional dish I remember from my childhood. This is wonderful teatime fare but can also be served for breakfast. My mother remembers going to the meal shop in Dundee before her mother fried herring for tea. This was where most Dundonians would buy their oatmeal in different grades (medium, pinhead, coarse, fine) for dishes varying from porridge to fried herring. It also sold dried pulses.

Because herring is best between early June and September in Scotland, fried herring is often served with boiled new potatoes – preferably dug straight from the garden – for a true taste of summer.

You can use pinhead or medium oatmeal: pinhead gives a crunchier texture but medium coats more evenly.

Serves 2
50–65g/2–2½oz medium or pinhead
oatmeal
4 boned herrings (about 100g/3½oz each,
after boning)
or 2 trout fillets
25–40g/1–1½oz butter

Spread the oatmeal out on a large plate and season with salt and pepper, then press the fish into it, turning to coat both sides. If the fish has been freshly filleted for you, the oatmeal should stick well, but if it has been done earlier in the day, swish it briefly under a cold tap and shake dry before coating it in the meal. Heat the butter in a frying pan, then add the fish, flesh-side down. After about 3 minutes, turn it over and fry for another 3 minutes or until cooked through. Serve with new potatoes and lemon wedges or mustard.

Kipper Pâté

Although the kipper originated in the north-east of England, Scotland is also famous for its kippers. Most of the best ones are cured along the west coast – Loch Fyne, Achiltibuie or Mallaig – where plump herring have been fished for many years. Good ones are also available in the north-east of Scotland, where a fishmonger from Buckie, called Edward Mair (whose shop is called Eat Mair Fish), told me that Scottish kippers are incomparable in flavour because they are smoked over oak shavings from whisky barrels. It is this, he says, that makes Scottish kippers unique. His most certainly are.

Serves 6–8
2 large kippers
75g/3oz unsalted butter, softened
1 tablespoon Worcestershire sauce
juice of 1 lemon
a pinch of cayenne pepper (optional)

Place the kippers in a bowl, cover with boiling water and leave for 1 hour, then drain and pat dry. Peel away the skin and place the flesh in a food processor, discarding the bones. Add the butter, Worcestershire sauce and lemon juice and process until blended (the mixture does not have to be too smooth – a little texture is always welcome in potted fish or meat). Add the cayenne, if using, and some salt and pepper to taste. Pack into a small bowl and chill.

To serve, spread on hot toasted muffins or oat bannocks.

Crappit Heid

Crappit heid means stuffed head, and food writer F. Marian McNeill described it as a 'piscatorial haggis'. It was Rhoda Macleod, who now lives on Harris but was brought up on Lewis, who told me all about crappit heid, which she knows by the Gaelic name, *ceann cropaig*. She explained that first you need a very fresh fish. You must clean the liver thoroughly, then mash it with oatmeal with your hands before stuffing it into the head and boiling. She also sometimes steams the liver mixture in a bowl and discards the head, or makes *marag iasg* (fish pudding) from the mashed-up liver (no oatmeal) by packing it into the cleaned fish gullet and boiling it like a black or white pudding.

Rhoda also makes sheep's head broth (*ceann caorach*) by singeing the head, removing the eyes and splitting the head in half. After soaking in salt water overnight, it is rinsed, the brains are smeared all over it (to remove the taste of singeing) and then it is boiled to make a fine broth with turnips, carrots, onion and barley. None of this is for the faint-hearted.

Another Hebridean, Hamish Taylor of east Harris, told me he makes small fishcakes from the liver but he prefers to use coley rather than cod, since there are fewer worms. After washing the fish liver well, he mashes equal quantities of liver and wholemeal flour (again with the hands – their heat helps release the fish oil, which binds the mixture) and drops little cakes of the mixture into simmering water to poach.

Regional variations of crappit heid include stappit heidies in Caithness, Banff and Aberdeenshire, and krappin in Shetland. The latter is the mixture that is stuffed into a fish head or sometimes into a fish stomach (a 'muggie') to become krappit muggie. There is reference to fishermen taking fish-liver oatcake sandwiches to sea as their 'piece'. Who needs pastrami on rye anyway ...?

Although this dish would not win in the beauty stakes, it is truly delicious and well worth the rather arduous preparation. And you have all that lovely poaching broth to convert into fish soup afterwards.

Serves 6
1 cod's head, about 2kg/4½lb (cleaned weight)
1 cod's liver, about 600g/1¼lb (cleaned weight)
medium oatmeal
parsley or watercress, to garnish (optional)

First you have to clean the cod's head, which I ask my fishmonger to do for me. Remove the gills, then all the innards come out easily. Leave the lugs on (see Cabbie-claw on page 46), as these make ideal flaps to close over the stuffing. The eyes should be removed through the back, to give you perfect sockets; if you cut them out from the front, there will be tendons left in. Now wash it all out and dry well.

Now tackle the liver. Cod's liver invariably has lots of tiny worms in it, so these should be removed. The easiest way is just to snip away with a sharp knife – or use your fingers. The worms are creamy white little rings. They are easier to remove than you might think, as they are all on the surface so most come away as you pull at the outer skin. Once all the worms are out, wash the liver thoroughly and pat dry.

Place the liver in a large bowl with an equal weight of oatmeal and season well. The fun begins now, as you must get in with your hands and squish everything together until it is thoroughly mixed. Then stuff the head: I find it easiest to position the head in the large pan you are to cook it in, then push in the stuffing, remembering to lift the lugs and tuck some in beside the cheeks. You can pack it quite tightly. Close over the flaps to cover but don't worry if the stuffing is not all enclosed. Pour over about 1.8 litres/3 pints of cold water (which will come most of the way up the head) and bring slowly to the boil. Then skim off any scum, cover and cook gently for 30 minutes. Take off the heat, remove any scum and allow to cool in the liquid, still covered, until warm, not hot.

Transfer the head carefully to an ashet (platter) and, if you like, decorate with some greenery such as parsley or watercress. My fishmonger suggests (tongue in cheek) inserting a couple of large kalamata olives into the eye sockets! The broth can be used as the base for a simple fish soup. When you serve, ensure everyone has a bit of the delicacies — tongue and cheek — as well as some stuffing.

Hairy Tatties

Hairy tatties — a mixture of mashed potatoes and salt fish — are a speciality of Aberdeenshire, where they are eaten with oatcakes and cold milk. There is another Scots dish called freckled tatties — baked sliced potatoes layered with fried onions, milk and ground pepper — which can be served, like the French *gratin dauphinois*, with roasts or steaks. Leftover hairy tatties can be shaped into fishballs or cakes, dipped in egg and breadcrumbs or oatmeal and fried until golden brown.

Serves 4–6
600–700g/1¼–1½lb salt cod
1.5kg/3lb 5oz floury potatoes, peeled and cut into chunks
100g/3½oz butter
200ml/7fl oz hot full-fat milk
2 heaped teaspoons Dijon mustard
2 tablespoons chopped parsley
2 free-range eggs, hard-boiled and sliced

Soak the cod in cold water for 24 hours, changing the water 2 or 3 times (more often if you know it is a heavy salt cure).

Put the cod in a pan, cover with fresh cold water and bring slowly to the boil. Reduce to a simmer, cover the pan and cook slowly for 5 minutes, then remove the fish and drain well. Leave until cool enough to handle, then flake the flesh into chunks, carefully removing skin and bones.

Boil the potatoes until tender, then drain well. Mash with the butter and milk and stir in the mustard and some pepper to taste (no salt). Fold in the flaked fish, then top with the parsley and slices of hard-boiled egg just before serving.

Hot-buttered Arbroath Smokies

The Arbroath smokie was first recorded in Arbroath Abbey's land register in 1178, as a gift from King William to the monks, though it is probable that it dates back even further. They were originally made in Auchmithie, three miles north of Arbroath, and it was only when fishermen from Auchmithie were enticed to migrate to Arbroath and its new harbour in the 1880s that the fisherfolk moved, taking with them the secret of their unique hot-smoked haddock.

To make Arbroath smokies, the haddock are gutted, beheaded, lightly brined and then hot-smoked in pairs, tied together by their tails, until just cooked. The smoking used to be done in barrels sunk into the ground. The haddock were hung from wooden poles over beech or oak chips, then damp hessian bags were placed over the top. Depending on the size of the fish, they would need only 30–45 minutes' smoking before emerging a gorgeous bronzed, tarry colour with soft, succulent, delicately flavoured flesh. These days, the smoking is done in more or less the same way but by commercial companies, on a larger scale.

My parents remember the Arbroath and Auchmithie fishwives, in their distinctive navy blue flannel skirts ('coats') and plaid shawls, coming to Dundee to sell fish from willow creels – mainly smokies but also Finnan haddie. My brother-in-law's grandmother, Isabella (Ise) Smith, was one of Arbroath's last fishwives to do this. Once a week, she travelled all the way from Arbroath to Perthshire to sell fish to the 'big houses' there. She was away for the entire day, most of which was spent travelling, by train to Perth, then bus. Amazingly she continued until she was nearly 70 years old, which was in the late 1960s – not so long ago.

This recipe is for the simplest way to enjoy a smokie. But they can, of course, be eaten cold in salads (because they are hot-smoked, they are completely cooked), whizzed into pâtés or mousses, or made into quiches or soufflés.

Serves 2
1 pair of Arbroath smokies
40g/1½oz butter, softened

Preheat the oven to 180°C/350°F/Gas 4. Remove the bone from each smokie. The easiest way to do this is to place the fish on a board, skin-side down, then press with your thumb along the length of the bone to release it. Gently pull and the whole bone should come away.

Place the boned smokies side by side on a large sheet of foil. Dice the butter and smear it over the insides. Close up and wrap the fish in the foil and bake for 15–20 minutes or until piping hot.

Place each smokie on a warm plate and pour over the buttery juices. Serve with either a baked potato or some rough country bread to soak up the juices. A salad on the side would be nice but, of course, is not traditional.

Arbroath Smokie Pancakes

This is one of many easy dishes you can make with the versatile smokie. When Margaret Horn cooks this in Auchmithie's But 'n' Ben, she makes a delicious soup with the skin and bones (remember, most of the flavour from the smoking is in the skin), boiling them up with water and flavourings such as onion, bay and peppercorns. After half an hour or so, this is strained and leeks, potatoes and other vegetables are simmered in it to make a soup. Towards the end of cooking, I like to add a good handful of lovage, which complements the smokie flavour well.

The easiest way to remove the flesh from smokies is to heat them briefly either in a low oven for 10 minutes or in a microwave for 2–3 minutes.

Serves 4
300ml/10fl oz double cream
3 medium smokies
(or 2 small pairs, i.e. 4 small smokies)

For the pancakes:
225g/8oz plain flour, sifted
3 medium free-range eggs
350ml/12fl oz full-fat milk
a little butter for frying

First make the pancake batter: place the flour, eggs and milk in a food mixer or processor and process until smooth. Or beat together by hand until smooth. Pour into a wide jug and chill for an hour or so. To make the pancakes, smear the base of a crêpe pan with a little butter, then, once hot, add 2 tablespoons of the batter and swirl it around to cover the base of the pan. Once the underside is done, flip over and cook the other side (2–3 minutes altogether). Stack the pancakes in a pile. This amount should make 12.

For the filling, bring the cream slowly to the boil in a saucepan and cook over a medium heat for a couple of minutes until slightly thickened. Season well with pepper. Remove the flesh from the smokies and, ensuring it is bone-free, add it to the pan. Stir for a minute or so, then remove from the heat. Place a spoonful of the mixture in each pancake and roll up. If the pancakes are still hot, serve at once; otherwise tuck them into an ovenproof dish, side by side, and cover with foil. Heat gently in an oven preheated to 180°C/350°F/Gas 4 for about 15 minutes or until piping hot.

Cullen Skink Tart

The idea for this tart came from my visit to Alan McPherson's bakery in Cullen to see how butteries are made. As Alan was kneading and shaping the butteries, Derek the pie man poured a thick cullen skink mixture into dinky little pastry cases for his cullen skink pies. Here is my version – a thinner tart, made with a polenta or oatmeal pastry. I serve it warm with salad.

Serves 6–8
1 small onion, peeled and chopped
1 medium potato, peeled and diced
25g/1oz butter
400g/14oz undyed smoked haddock fillets
300ml/10fl oz full-fat milk
3 medium free-range eggs
2 tablespoons chopped parsley or lovage

For the pastry:
200g/7oz plain flour, sifted
25g/1oz fine oatmeal or polenta
125g/4½oz butter, diced
1 large free-range egg
1 teaspoon olive oil

For the pastry, place the flour, oatmeal or polenta and butter in a food processor, then add the egg and oil and process briefly. (Alternatively, put the dry ingredients in a bowl, rub in the butter, then mix to a dough with the egg and oil.) Wrap in clingfilm and chill for an hour or so. Roll out and use to line a buttered 28cm/11in loose-bottomed flan tin. Prick all over with a fork and chill again. Preheat the oven to 190°C/375°F/Gas 5.

Line the pastry case with foil, fill with baking beans and bake for 15 minutes. Remove the foil and beans and bake for a further 5 minutes, then leave to cool.

Sauté the onion and potato in the butter until tender, then set aside. Poach the fish in the milk for 3–4 minutes, then strain over a jug and break the fish into chunks. Beat the strained milk with the eggs, herbs and some seasoning. Place the onion, potato and fish in the pastry case. Pour in the liquid and bake for 30–35 minutes or until golden brown. Serve warm.

shellfish and crustaceans

4

It is extraordinary to think that until relatively recently, the consumption of shellfish went hand in hand with poverty. Oysters were eaten daily by the poor. It is recorded that in early-nineteenth-century Edinburgh (a much smaller city than today) some 100,000 oysters were consumed every single day. Lobster and crab were so cheap that they were daily fare in coastal villages and were eaten particularly in times of scarcity. Other molluscs, such as mussels, which we nowadays make into glorious stews and soups, were used only as bait.

How times have changed. Apart from mussels, which are still fairly inexpensive, most shellfish are now regarded as a luxury item. This is partly because industrial pollution spoiled shellfish beds in the shallow waters, resulting in fishermen going further afield; also, at long last we Scots – and, it seems, the rest of the British Isles – have woken up to the fact that shellfish are absolutely delicious.

The recipes in this chapter are incredibly simple, as befits some of the finest ingredients in the world. So Hebridean clamcakes are simply scallops (often called clams in the Hebrides) coated in oatmeal and fried. Stewed oysters are those fabulous molluscs sautéed very lightly in butter and served on thick slices of toast. Mussels in a bag are mussels cooked in foil parcels over a peat fire or, for those sultry summer days, a barbecue.

Two lobster recipes show how versatile that beast is. The more sophisticated one includes an adaptation of Lady Clark of Tillypronie's mayonnaise sauce for lobster. The other is Margaret Horn's chew and spit lobster, which is just that: boiled lobster attacked with lobster picks and fingers, the meat chewed, then any pieces of shell spat out. Just as sublime as Lady Clark's dish but definitely more 'hands-on' – perhaps more suited to kitchen supper than dining-room dinner.

If you are nervous about preparing shellfish yourself, do not overlook these recipes, for your fishmonger is there to help. If no help is forthcoming, change shops and go to the one down the road.

Mussel and Onion Stew

The garlic in this delicious and simple stew is not authentic but I think it enhances the whole dish. Serve this with plenty of crusty bread to dunk into the juices.

Serves 4

1kg/2¼lb mussels

2–3 sprigs of thyme

400ml/14fl oz dry white wine

40g/1½oz butter

2 onions, peeled and chopped

2 large garlic cloves, peeled and chopped

40g/1½oz parsley, chopped

Scrub the mussels thoroughly, discarding any open ones that don't close when tapped on a work surface. Place them in a large pan with the thyme sprigs and white wine, cover tightly and bring slowly to the boil. Boil for about 1 minute, until the shells have opened, then remove from the heat and strain over a jug. Discard any mussels that have not opened.

Heat the butter in the pan in which the mussels were cooked and gently fry the onions and garlic in it for about 10 minutes, until softened. Increase the heat and add the mussel liquor. Bring to the boil and bubble away for 4–5 minutes to reduce a little, then taste and season accordingly. Return the mussels to the pan in their shells. Stir gently and warm through over a low heat for a minute or so, then scatter over the parsley. Ladle into warm bowls and serve immediately.

Chew and Spit Lobster

When Margaret Horn was growing up in the tiny coastal village of Auchmithie in Angus, chew and spit lobster and crab were everyday summer fare. She was a child during the Second World War, when the lobster pots set down in the harbour were full most days. But because the lobsters could not easily be sent to the country's smart restaurants, many were consumed locally. Margaret remembers shortly after the war being taken to dinner in Edinburgh by her husband-to-be and ordering lobster. It was only when she saw his face – and later the bill – that she realised that lobster was a luxury everywhere else.

The whole family would sit down to a tray in the middle of the table bearing freshly boiled lobsters and crabs, accompanied only by some bread and butter (no lemon wedges in those days), then proceed to tuck in with their hands. There were no forks used – and absolutely no finesse, which is why Margaret's family called it chew and spit lobster. The meat was prodded and poked out with the ends of teaspoons, then the claws and legs sucked dry of their juices, and any tiny pieces of shell were spat out.

When you eat lobster in this manner, with only some bread and a glass of chilled white wine (milk or water when Margaret was a child) you begin to appreciate that the best things in life are often the simplest. No adornments of mayonnaise or the complication of thermidor are required. Just plenty of time and patience. And finger bowls if you absolutely must.

Serves 2
1 live lobster, weighing
600–700g/1¼–1½lb
lemon wedges (optional)

Place the lobster in the freezer for a couple of hours to chill it into unconsciousness before boiling, as recommended by the RSPCA. Then bring a large pan of salted water to the boil, plunge the lobster in head first and, using tongs, keep it immersed for at least 2 minutes, then allow the water to return to the boil. Counting from when the water returns to a full boil, cook for 15 minutes. Lobsters over 700g/1½lb will require 20 minutes; ones over 1.1kg/2½lb, will need 25 minutes. Remove the lobster, place on a board and leave to cool.

Once it is cool enough to handle (it is easier to extract the flesh if the lobster is still a little warm), twist off the main claws and remove the rubber bands binding them. Lay the lobster on a board, shell uppermost, pull back the tail to extend the body and, with a sharp knife, cut down the middle, all along the length of the lobster. You might need to give it a few sharp taps as you go. Remove and discard the inedible stomach sac (which looks like crumpled clingfilm), the dark intestinal thread running down the tail and the greyish, feathery gills.

And now everything you see is edible. Squeeze over some lemon juice, if you like. If it is a hen lobster, you have the bonus of eating the coral. Bash the claws to open them, or simply poke at them with a lobster pick or skewer to remove the meat. Then remove the main tail meat in one piece. Continue by sucking at the legs to extract every last morsel of meat. Nibble on some brown bread and butter and slurp a chilled glass of fine white burgundy or champagne. Your hands will now be covered in lobster bits and pieces and reek of crustacea. But then so are your dinner partner's. And besides, when you are indulging in one of life's sweetest pleasures, table manners go by the board.

Potted Crab

This recipe is versatile: it can be chilled and served in little ramekins or served hot, straight from the pan. The latter is one of Clarissa Dickson Wright's great party dishes. Both ways are delicious, provided you use the best ingredients. Only freshly cooked crabmeat should be used, never tinned.

Serves 4
75g/3oz unsalted butter
250g/9oz freshly boiled crabmeat (white and brown)
scant ½ teaspoon ground mace
juice of ½ lemon
a pinch of cayenne pepper

Melt the butter in a saucepan then add the crabmeat, mace, lemon juice and cayenne. Heat gently for 8–10 minutes, then taste and add salt and pepper accordingly.

Either serve warm from the pan or pour into 4 ramekins and chill until set – preferably overnight. Eat with warm toast or oatcakes.

Scallops with Mash

This is not a traditional recipe but it is the type of dish chefs are serving up more and more: local produce cooked in a straightforward way. Delicious, yet very simple.

The scallops are also wonderful served with a pea mash made by puréeing 250g/9oz fresh or frozen peas – just cooked – with half the butter and them mixing them with the potatoes. Add some chopped fresh mint to make it even more special.

The reason you should separate the scallop muscle from the coral before cooking is that the coral requires less cooking and it tends to burst and splutter in a very hot pan if cooked for too long. Smaller scallops can be left whole.

Serves 4

12 plump, fresh scallops,
(ensure they have not been frozen)
olive oil
1kg/2¼lb floury potatoes
(e.g. Maris Piper, Desiree, King Edward),
peeled and chopped
100g/3½oz butter
100ml/3½fl oz hot full-fat milk

Separate the scallop muscle (which is white) from the coral (which is orange). Marinate both muscle and coral in a little olive oil, turning until well covered. Leave for 20 minutes or so.

Meanwhile, cook the potatoes in boiling salted water until tender, then drain well. Mash with the butter and milk and season well with salt and pepper. For the scallops, heat a good solid frying pan until very hot, then add the scallop muscles (which because of their marinade require no further oil). Season with salt and pepper, cook for 1 minute and then turn Add the scallop corals and cook for 1–2 minutes, until both muscle and coral are cooked – just.

To serve, place a mound of mash in the centre of each plate and top with the scallops and the coral.

Hebridean Clamcakes

These are not clams but scallops, which are known as clams on some Hebridean islands. They are simply coated in oatmeal and fried until crunchy outside, soft and tender inside. Delicious.

This recipe uses only the scallop muscle. Instead of discarding the corals, I like to poach them gently in a little fish stock (about a cupful for the 6 corals), then whizz them up in a blender with seasoning and serve with the clamcakes.

Serves 2 as a starter

6 plump, fresh scallops, trimmed, corals carefully cut off
1 medium free-range egg, beaten
75g/3oz medium oatmeal
25g/1oz butter

Dip the scallops in the beaten egg, then coat in the oatmeal. Chill for an hour or so, then dip in egg again and re-coat in oatmeal. Chill again. Bring the scallops to room temperature for 15–20 minutes before cooking.

Heat the butter in a frying pan until medium-hot, then fry the scallops for 2–3 minutes on each side, until just done. Serve piping hot.

Stewed Oysters

'I ate some excellent oysters at the table of this learned man [a Doctor in Prestonpans, east of Edinburgh] as was not to be wondered at, seeing that I was in the place where the most famous oysters are taken in abundance; the rocks at the surface of the sea around the coast are covered with them. They are large, plump and of an exquisite taste; and are held in such estimation, that they are exported to the principal cities of England and Holland.' Thus wrote B. Faujas de Saint-Fond in *A Journey Through England and Scotland to the Hebrides in 1784*. For, up until the twentieth century, oysters were not only plentiful, they were cheap. In the 1880s some 1,200 million oysters a year were eaten in Britain, according to *The Story of Loch Fyne Oysters* by Christina Noble. She describes how in Edinburgh's elegant New Town, the Oyster Lassies from Newhaven went around calling, 'Wha'l o caller ou?' ('Who'll have fresh oysters?') Their dress – rather like the Arbroath and Auchmithie fish wives – was distinctive, with dark blue jacket, striped petticoats and a basket creel full of oysters on their back.

There are several old recipes for cooked oysters and one that often crops up is oyster loaves – stewed oysters served in a hot bread roll or small loaf. The following recipe can be served in this way, or – my favourite – on thick slices of hot buttered toast.

Loch Fyne is probably the most famous place in the country for oysters these days. Pacific or rock oysters (*Crassostrea gigas*) have been farmed in this sea loch for some years now. Available all year, they have a superb flavour and are also relatively cheap. If, however, you can get your hands on native oysters (*Ostrea edulis*), these are the ones to savour raw (it would be a sacrilege to cook them; besides they are expensive) – with a pile of fresh brown bread and butter, a wedge or two of lemon and a glass of champagne, chilled white wine or Guinness. The latter is not exactly Scottish, I know, but the combination is truly perfect. And as for those scaremongers who insist that whisky, brandy or any spirits should never

be drunk with oysters . . . There is no reason why a glass of peaty malt whisky should not accompany oysters if you wish. I personally like claret with this dish; Leith (famous for the centuries-old claret trade) is, after all, the next port along the coast from Newhaven.

Serves 2
a dozen oysters in their shells
40g/1½oz butter
a little white wine
thick toast or hot rolls, to serve

First shuck the oysters: wrap your left hand in a tea towel (assuming you are right handed) and place an oyster, cup-side down, hinge towards you, in your palm. Insert an oyster knife or small sharp knife into the hinge. Push and twist simultaneously, passing the knife under the top shell to cut the muscle and sliding it along the length to open fully. Remove the oyster from its shell, retaining all the juices.

Melt the butter in a large frying pan and toss in the oysters and any juices with plenty of black pepper (you don't need salt). Sauté them very briefly – for about 2 minutes – just until they are warm, then add a splash of wine and remove from the heat.

Serve on thick slices of hot buttered toast or in individual hot rolls (top sliced off, insides scooped out, and heated in a hot oven for 5 minutes). Eat at once – perhaps with an improbable-sounding glass of claret, in true Edinburgh style!

Dods Macfarlane's Mussels in a Bag

Dods Macfarlane has lived in the port of Ness on the Butt of Lewis all his life. For most of the year he sells fresh and salt herring, mackerel, smoked haddock, cod and ling. Every summer, however, he and nine other men of Ness make a voyage to a remote rock in the Atlantic, Sula Sgeir, some 40 miles north of Lewis, to harvest guga, as part of a legacy that has existed for some four centuries.

Gugas are plump young gannets, 2,000 of which are harvested every year. Although they are protected birds, a statutory order inserted into the 1954 Protection of Birds Act allows Nessmen to continue the tradition of hunting them. Once the men arrive on the tiny island they set up camp, then spend 14 days catching the birds, which involves remarkable rock-climbing skills, usually amid the most adverse weather conditions. After being killed, the birds are decapitated, plucked, singed, dewinged and split. They are then salted and piled in a mound (a 'pickling stack') with a wheel formation. When the men return home to Ness with their harvest, they are met on the quay by a queue of locals, all eager to buy a pair of gugas, which will be desalinated, boiled and eaten with potatoes. It is one of Dods' favourite dishes – the taste often described as neither fish nor fowl, but somewhere between steak and kipper. Last year Dods took a barbecue to Sula Sgeir, amid much teasing from his fellow hunters. In the morning he marinated some guga in HP sauce before barbecuing them that night. He insists it was absolutely delicious.

And an equally delicious – but more accessible – Dods dish is mussels wrapped in foil and thrown on to a peat fire. He adds no flavours as he says that there are enough juices in the mussels. Since few of us have peat fires, I recommend cooking the mussels on a barbecue. And I also suggest some supplementary flavourings. Sorry Dods.

Serves 4
24–28 large mussels
a little oil

Optional flavourings:
3–4 spring onions, chopped
2 teaspoons grated fresh root ginger
2 garlic cloves, peeled and chopped
2 tablespoons white wine
2 tablespoons olive oil

Scrub the mussels well, discarding any open ones that don't close when tapped on a work surface. Cut 4 pieces of foil about 30cm/12in square and place on a work surface. Lightly oil them, then place the spring onions, ginger and garlic, if using, on each one. Top with the mussels, then divide the wine and oil between them, if using. Crimp the edges of the foil together to seal, then place the parcels either on a peat fire or on the hottest part of your barbecue for about 10 minutes, until the mussels have opened. Eat straight from the bag.

Grilled Lobster
with Lady Clark's Mayonnaise Sauce

Lady Clark of Tillypronie was an inveterate recipe collector, with an unusual (for that time) curiosity about food. She would ask cooks in the houses she dined in for recipes then have her own cooks prepare them in her home in north-east Scotland. After she died, a cookbook was compiled from her collection as a memorial, requested by her husband. Her mayonnaise sauce recipe for lobster, crab or crayfish is enlivened with mustard, gherkins and capers. She also stirred in some thick cream at the end. I prefer adding yoghurt to thin it down slightly and sharpen the flavour, although it is wonderful served as it is – thick and glossy, without any embellishment.

It is worth heeding Lady Clark's advice about mayonnaise: 'To be well made this requires much care.' Mayonnaise is hard work by hand, as you have to whisk continually while drizzling in the oil, but for such a small quantity I find it is not worth dirtying the food processor. If you feel safer using a machine, however, you should probably double the quantities, as this amount is too small for most food processors.

Serves 2
1 live lobster, weighing 600–700g/1¼–1½lb

For the mayonnaise:
1 medium free-range egg yolk
½ teaspoon Dijon mustard
150ml/5fl oz oil (I use half olive, half sunflower)
1 tablespoon chopped mixed capers and gherkins
1 tablespoon Greek yoghurt (optional)

First make the mayonnaise: put the egg yolk and mustard into a bowl and place it on a damp cloth to stop it slipping. Whisk until combined. Now add the oil – literally drop by drop at first – whisking all the time until it thickens. After you have added about a third of the oil, add the rest in a very thin stream, whisking continuously. Once all the oil has been added, stir in the capers and gherkins, and the yoghurt if using. Season to taste with salt and pepper.

Now prepare the lobster in the same way as for Chew and Spit Lobster (see page 60), but boil (once the water has returned to a full boil) for only 5 minutes. Cool, split in half, remove the stomach sac and dark intestinal tract. Don't worry if you see green slime – it is the liver (called the tomalley) which is edible. If it is a female lobster, remove the coral and add it to the mayonnaise. (If you prefer, you could grill the lobster without par-boiling: cut it in half when you remove it from the freezer by pushing a sharp knife through the well-defined cross on the back of the head and quickly splitting it in half lengthwise down the back. Remove the stomach and intestinal tract.) Twist off the claws (removing the rubber bands), brush them with oil and cook for about 5 minutes over a medium barbecue or under a grill.

Brush oil all over the body section, then place the halves, shell-side down on a barbecue or under a grill, shell-side up for 8–10 minutes. Turn and cook, flesh-side down on a barbecue, flesh-side up – towards the heat – under a grill for about 2–3 minutes or until just done. You will need 15–20 minutes altogether (an extra 5 minutes) if the lobster has not been par-boiled.

Serve the warm lobster with the mayonnaise sauce.

5

meat and poultry

'Some hae meat and canna eat
And some wad eat that want it
But we hae meat and we can eat
Sae let the Lord be thankit.'

Robert Burns' famous Selkirk Grace sums it up really. Meat has always been of prime importance in Scotland. Whether eaten on high days and holidays or as everyday fare, it has always been revered – until the introduction of intensive farming. Gradually many people began to eat less meat, because of the resulting inferior quality and because of the concomitant food scares and welfare issues. I believe red meat is a valuable addition to the diet, with its high iron content and vitamins. Ironically, though, many consumers gave up red meat and opted for white meat such as chicken, which although also good for you, is the meat most likely to have been inhumanely reared in cramped conditions.

But it was not always thus. And thankfully meat eaters in Scotland and elsewhere are welcoming the return of extensive, often organic, farming, not only on welfare grounds but also because the meat tastes better. Some old-fashioned dishes such as stoved howtowdie simply would not work with battery chicken, with its flabby, wet flesh. It requires a sturdy, firm chicken, whose life has involved plenty of activity.

Scottish beef and lamb are some of the finest in the world (you will notice that pork does not come into the equation, as we Scots have always harboured an innate aversion to pork, apart from bacon and ham). And when you see great, lumbering Aberdeen Angus standing proud in a field of lush green grass in Aberdeenshire, or Cheviot sheep nibbling their way along a dry-stane dyke in the Borders, you begin to appreciate that Scottish meat is inherently free-range in the true sense of the word.

A joint of Scottish beef – from a reliable butcher who not only hangs his meat well but also assures you it is from traditionally reared, grass-fed cattle – is a memorable feast. A leg of Borders, Shetland or Hebridean lamb, simply roasted, is another sublime dish. In this chapter, there are, of course, some embellishments to basic roasts, stews and mince but, provided you have top-quality meat, I like to do as Escoffier advised and '*Faites simple*' – keep it simple.

Mince and Tatties

'Yes, but can she cook mince?' A young Scotsman extolling the beauty and talents of his intended bride to his family was invariably asked this question. Mince is such an important dish in Scotland that it is virtually written into the wedding contract. My mother reckons she ate it at least three days a week when she was a child. And with the mince it was always tatties. Occasionally, if you were very lucky, there might be a green vegetable, too, but more likely it was a tin of peas or beans. We Scots did not acquire our anti-vegetable reputation for nothing. In Aberdeenshire, a white (mealie) pudding is placed over the mince for the last 15–20 minutes or so of cooking and is called mince and mealies. If you do this, don't worry if the pudding bursts as this only enhances the flavour of the mince.

My mother's basic recipe is to brown the mince in a little dripping, add chopped onion and water then simmer until cooked, thickening at the end with Bisto. Instead of Bisto I either crumble in some stock cube or add a little Marmite for a good savoury flavour. A shake of Worcestershire sauce is not traditional but my family likes it. You could also add mushroom ketchup if you can find it.

The good flavour comes from using only the best-quality mince, preferably steak minced in front of you at the butcher's. If you know it is not terribly lean, then do not use any fat to brown it; just place it in a very hot pan on its own. As for the texture, it should be soft enough to dribble seductively over your mound of mash but thick enough to make a decent forkful. The derogatory Scottish expression, 'thick as mince', did not arrive on the linguistic scene by chance.

Serves 4

a knob of dripping or butter

500g/18oz best beef mince

1 medium or ½ large onion, peeled and finely chopped

½ beef stock cube or 1 teaspoon Marmite

Worcestershire sauce or mushroom ketchup (optional)

Champit Tatties (see page 112), to serve

Heat the dripping or butter in a solid, reliable pan, then add the mince and brown over a high heat, stirring around to break it up. This should take about 5 minutes. Add the onion, crumble in the stock cube or stir in the Marmite and season with some salt and pepper. Add 3–4 tablespoons of boiling water, stir well, then cover and cook over a medium heat for about 20 minutes. Add a good shake of Worcestershire sauce or mushroom ketchup if required, then check the seasoning again. Serve piping hot with the tatties and some freshly cooked peas or stir-fried cabbage.

Potted Hough

Similar to English brawn, which is made with pork, potted hough is a traditional dish that uses up cheaper cuts of beef. The word 'hough' (pronounced hoch, as in loch) means shin and it is this meat that is boiled up for hours until tender and gelatinous. It is then potted and served with salad or bread, although in my mother's family it was eaten in the summer with new potatoes and a vegetable such as cabbage or turnips, the warmth of the hot potatoes melting the jelly on top of the meat.

This version is based on my Auntie Bette's recipe. She only used salt and white pepper as seasoning, never spices, but I give these here as an optional extra. Auntie Bette also used to pot it in teacups to make individual servings.

Serves 6–8
900g/2lb hough (shin of beef)
1 knap (fore-nap) bone or knuckle, washed
½ teaspoon mace blade (optional)
½ teaspoon peppercorns (optional)
½ teaspoon whole allspice (optional)

Wipe the meat all over and place it in a large soup pot with the bone and cold water to cover – about 2.25 litres/4 pints. If using the mace, peppercorns and allspice, tie them in a piece of muslin and add to the pan. Cover tightly and simmer over a very low heat for about 5–6 hours, until the meat is very tender. Remove the bone and place the meat on a board. Strain the stock, remove the spice bag and add salt and pepper to the stock to taste.

Shred or finely chop the meat and return it to the stock pan. Bring back to the boil and boil for about 5 minutes, then remove. Pour the mixture into wetted moulds or bowls (rinsed in cold water) and leave until completely cold.

Meatroll

Meatroll (or meatloaf) recipes vary from region to region, and also in shape and size. My mother's was always round, made in a pottery meatroll 'jar'. In the north-east it is called Aberdeenshire sausage or roll and was often made in a round coffee tin.

My recipe is based on that of Mrs Doig, the minister's wife. My dear friend Isabelle Doig and I would always play together at the manse after school and I was usually asked to stay for tea. I always agreed, and especially enjoyed it if it was Mrs Doig's famous meatloaf. After tea, realising the time, I had to run home – arriving a little late – and sit down to a second tea. Sadly my appetite has not diminished much over the years.

Serves 6–8

450g/1lb lean minced beef
250g/9oz lean minced pork
75g/3oz fresh breadcrumbs
1 medium free-range egg
½ large onion, peeled and finely chopped
1 tablespoon Worcestershire sauce or
mushroom ketchup
1 tablespoon chopped parsley

Preheat the oven to 150°C/200°F/Gas 2. Mix everything together and season generously with salt and pepper. Spoon into a lightly buttered 900g/2lb loaf tin, pressing down well. Cover loosely with foil and bake for 1¾–2 hours. Leave to cool in the tin for at least 20 minutes, then carefully drain off any liquid and turn out on to a plate. Cut into thick slices and serve warm with a fresh tomato sauce and new potatoes or tagliatelle, or cold with salad and good crusty bread.

Stornoway Black Pudding and Potato Stack

The idea for this comes from Roddy Aflin, chef-proprietor at the Park Guest House in Stornoway, who uses butcher Iain Macleod's wonderful black pudding. He serves it as a starter with a red wine reduction flavoured with oil and vinegar, but I like to serve it with a simple balsamic vinegar and olive oil dressing. It is also divine without the dressing. Roddy uses sweet potato, which looks good, but it tastes superb with ordinary potato, too.

Serves 4

16 x 1cm/½in slices of black pudding
(preferably Stornoway pudding), skinned
16 x 5mm/¼in slices of potato
or sweet potato
melted butter for brushing
2 tablespoons extra virgin olive oil
1 tablespoon balsamic vinegar

Place the black pudding and potato slices on a sheet of foil and brush with melted butter, then season with salt and pepper. Place under a preheated grill for 3 minutes, then turn the potatoes over. Remove the black pudding after 2 minutes (so they are cooked for 5 minutes altogether) and keep warm – and continue to cook the potato slices until done – about 7–8 minutes altogether.

To assemble, stack up alternative slices of black pudding and potato on each plate, starting with black pudding and finishing with a potato slice, seasoning with a little salt between the layers. Whisk together the oil and vinegar with a little seasoning and drizzle or dot this dressing over and around the stack. Serve at once.

Musselburgh Pie

In Musselburgh (the 'Honest Toun'), situated to the east of Edinburgh on the Firth of Forth, there have been oyster and mussel beds for many centuries. Clarissa Dickson Wright, in her charming book, *Hieland Foodie*, writes that these beds have been harvested since Roman times. Native British oysters, which were highly prized by the Romans, were transported in seaweed-lined barrels to the emperor's table in Rome.

In the days when they were literally two a penny, many of the oysters for Edinburgh's oyster bars came from the shoreline around Musselburgh. Now it is a polluted coastline, but this Musselburgh pie recipe, which combines oysters with rump steak, is a delightful remembrance of things past.

Serves 4

6 very thin slices of rump steak
(called popeseye steak in Scotland),
weighing about 750g/1lb 10oz in total
12 oysters
1 heaped tablespoon flour, seasoned with
salt and pepper
50g/2oz butter
2 onions, peeled and chopped
250ml/9fl oz boiling beef stock
about 250g/9oz ready-rolled puff pastry
beaten egg, to glaze

Preheat the oven to 170°C/325°F/Gas 3. Cut the steak slices in half and lay them on a board. Open the oysters (see page 65), remove them from their shells and reserve the juices. Wrap each oyster in a piece of beef and dip them in the seasoned flour. Place in a 1.5 litre/2½ pint pie dish; they should fit snugly. Season well.

Heat the butter in a saucepan, add the onions and fry until tender, then tip them over the beef. Pour over the oyster juices and the boiling stock. Cover very tightly and cook in the oven for 1½ hours, then leave to cool completely.

Preheat the oven to 220°C/425°F/Gas 7. Cut a long strip off the rolled-out pastry. Wet your fingers lightly and dampen the edges of the pie dish. Place the pastry strip round the rim of the dish, then brush with some of the beaten egg. Place the remaining pastry over the top and press down to seal all the edges. Trim off any excess pastry and crimp the edges between your thumb and forefinger. Brush with egg, slit the top to allow steam to escape and bake for about 25 minutes, until golden brown.

Forfar Bridies

Bridies and pies are still very much a part of life in Dundee and Angus. And whereas the best pies have traditionally come from Dundee, the best bridies are from Forfar.

According to F. Marian McNeill, the first Forfar bridie baker was a Mr Jolly in the mid-nineteenth century. My recipe is based on Bill McLaren's, whose great-grandfather, James McLaren, learned the skills of bridie-making at Jolly's bakery. His family-run bakery, opened in 1893, has baked bridies to the same recipe ever since. When I visited him there, he taught me the essential 'dunting' and 'nicking' procedure to seal the horseshoe-shaped bridie.

There are also some recipes for venison bridies, which could be even more ancient than the now-traditional beef, since deer roamed the Highlands long before cattle.

Makes 4
450g/1lb shoulder or rump of beef
75g/3oz beef suet, grated
1 small onion, peeled and finely grated

For the pastry:
250g/9oz strong white flour
75g/3oz plain flour
a pinch of salt
75g/3oz unsalted butter, diced
75g/3oz white fat, diced

For the pastry, sift the flours and salt into a food processor. Add the fats and process until incorporated. Add just enough cold water (2½–3 tablespoons) to bind to a stiff dough. Gather it up in your hands, wrap in clingfilm and chill for at least 1 hour.

For the filling, roughly chop the beef – I use the pulse button on my food processor – or mince it very coarsely. Mix together the beef, suet, onion and plenty of salt and pepper. The mixture should be fairly stiff. Divide the pastry into 4 and roll each piece into an oval. Spoon the filling on to one half of each pastry oval, leaving a border all round it. Dampen the edges of the pastry and fold the uncovered half over the filling to enclose it. Trim the edges into a neat horseshoe shape (not a half-moon: that is the Cornish pasty). Now 'dunt' it by pressing down on the edges with the heel of your hand and 'nick' it by crimping with your forefinger and thumb to give a nice finish. Using a sharp knife, prick a small hole (for steam to escape) in the top of each bridie. Place on a lightly buttered baking tray and chill for an hour or so. Preheat the oven to 200°C/400°F/Gas 6.

Bake the bridies for 35–40 minutes or until golden brown. Serve warm.

Steak Pie

Steak pie used to be the main course on New Year's Day – and indeed, often on Christmas Day (which was, of course, just another working day) – for my parents' families. The pies were seldom home-made but were bought from the butcher's shop. The reason for this was not only that people were simply too busy but also a good butcher's steak pie was – still is – a thing of great beauty, and delicious, too. The enamel ashet (dish) was taken to the butcher's to be filled and baked, then all it required was reheating at home before being served with mashed potatoes and marrowfat peas or butterbeans.

When I make a steak pie myself, I start it the day before so that the stew has time to cool down and thicken up a little before I cover it with the pastry. I like to serve it with mashed potatoes, stir-fried cabbage and Brussels sprouts or peas.

Serves 6
50g/2oz dripping or butter
900g/2lb stewing beef, diced (my butcher recommends chuck (shoulder) steak)
40g/1½oz plain flour, well seasoned with salt and pepper
1 large onion, peeled and chopped
4 large carrots, peeled and thickly sliced
600ml/1 pint hot beef stock
1 heaped tablespoon tomato purée
1 tablespoon Worcestershire sauce
250g/9oz ready-rolled puff pastry
beaten egg, to glaze

Heat the dripping or butter in a heavy saucepan. Toss half the meat in the seasoned flour and brown it all over in the fat, then remove with a slotted spoon. Toss the remaining meat in the flour and brown all over. Remove with a slotted spoon, then add the onion and carrots to the pan (if necessary, add a little extra fat at this stage). Fry gently for about 5 minutes, until softened, then return the meat to the pan with the hot stock, tomato purée and Worcestershire sauce. Grind in plenty of black pepper and some salt, stir well and bring to the boil. Then cover and reduce to a simmer. Cook very gently for 2 hours, stirring once, then check the seasoning. Tip into a 1.8 litre/3 pint pie dish and leave to cool completely. Cover and refrigerate overnight.

The next day, preheat the oven to 220°C/425°F/Gas 7. Cut a long strip off the rolled-out pastry. Wet your fingers lightly and dampen the edges of the pie dish. Place the pastry strip round the rim of the pie dish, then brush with some of the beaten egg. Place the remaining pastry over the top and press down to seal all the edges. Trim off any excess pastry and crimp the edges between your thumb and forefinger. Brush with more beaten egg and use scissors to snip a hole in the middle. Bake for 30–35 minutes, until puffed up and golden brown. You might need to lay a piece of foil lightly over the surface for the last 10 minutes or so to prevent burning. Serve piping hot.

Scotch Pies

Made from beef or mutton, these are small raised pies with a pastry lid that sits down a little inside the top of the rim. They are never referred to as Scotch pies, except in books. In Dundee they are simply called pies (pronounced 'peh'). They are crucial to the average Dundonian, and even those ex-pats living elsewhere will stock up on pies from Dundee butchers and bakers and freeze them. There is some rivalry between the two professions, bakers insisting their pastry is best, butchers insisting their filling is best. David Craig of Robertson's butcher's in Broughty Ferry has come to the best compromise by buying shells from one of Dundee's top bakers and filling them with his own top-quality meat. Pies were traditional Saturday lunchtime fare, eaten hot with beans or peas, presumably as a quick meal that freed the men for the football in the afternoon.

David Craig has given me the recipe for his famous pies, which are so popular with locals. He recommends freezing them uncooked if you don't want to bake them all at once. If you do not want to make the pastry yourself, many good bakers and butchers in Scotland sell Scotch pie shells.

Makes 15–20
700g/1½lb lean minced beef
300g/10½oz white rusks
(baby rusks are fine), crushed
25g/1oz seasoning, made of 3 parts salt to
1 part white pepper)
beaten egg, to glaze

For the pastry:
225g/8oz lard or dripping
700g/1½lb self-raising flour
1 teaspoon salt

For the pastry, put the fat in a pan with 300ml/10fl oz water and bring to the boil until the fat has melted. Sift the flour and salt into a warmed bowl (to take off the chill) and stir in the liquid. Work with a wooden spoon until cool enough to handle, then knead until smooth. Cover and leave in a warm place until firmed up a little but still pliable. Roll out to fit 15–20 pie moulds (or large, deep bun or muffin tins). Roll out the remaining pastry and cut out lids to fit your tins. Leave the pastry shells and lids somewhere cool to harden overnight.

Preheat the oven to 190°C/375°F/Gas 5. For the filling, mix the mince and rusks with enough ice-cold water to bind to a stiff consistency, then add the seasoning.

Fill the pie shells about three-quarters full (no more), then press in the lids and glaze with egg. Slit a tiny hole in each lid. Bake for about 25 minutes or until the pastry is golden brown and cooked through. Serve piping hot.

Hotchpotch

It was difficult to know whether to put this into the soup or meat chapter, for it is really something in between. Chunky and hearty, it is a thick soup or sloppy stew that requires only some bread or baked potatoes as an accompaniment.

Originally from the French word, *hochepot*, meaning a mutton, beef or fowl ragout with turnips and chestnuts, hotchpotch now means a dish of mixed ingredients, such as a stew with vegetables. Interestingly, there is a very similar rustic Dutch dish called *hutspot*, with almost the same ingredients.

My recipe is a modernised version of the old recipes, using lamb instead of mutton and as many vegetables as can be crammed in. I have left out the chestnuts, although they were extremely popular in Scotland in the past. The secret of a good hotchpotch is slow cooking, in order to have tender pieces of meat and a richly flavoured broth. If you dislike a fatty taste to your broth, cook the first stage (i.e. for 2 hours), then cool and chill. Scrape off surface fat and reheat to boiling before adding the remaining vegetables.

Serves 6
900g/2lb neck and/or shoulder of lamb (traditionally the bone is left in), chopped into very large pieces
8 carrots, peeled but left whole
600g/1¼lb baby turnips, peeled but left whole
1 large onion, peeled and cut into sixths or eighths
3–4 sprigs of thyme
4 large (or 8 medium) spring onions, trimmed
1 small cauliflower, cut into florets
3 heaped tablespoons chopped parsley

Place the meat in a large, heavy casserole. Top with 2 whole carrots, the whole turnips, onion and thyme. Cover with 1.2 litres/2 pints of cold water, add some salt and pepper and bring slowly to the boil. Skim off any scum from the surface, then cover and cook over a very low heat for about 2 hours (skim again if necessary.) Remove the vegetables and discard. Then bring the mixture up to the boil, add the remaining carrots, the whole spring onions and the cauliflower florets. Cook, covered, over a medium heat for about 15 minutes, until the vegetables are just tender. Check the seasoning and stir in the parsley. Using a slotted spoon, divide between deep plates or bowls.

Roast Beef with Cucumber and Ginger Salad

Although this cucumber salad may not seem a typically Scottish accompaniment to roast beef, the inspiration came from B. Faujas de Saint-Fond's journal, *A Journey through England and Scotland to the Hebrides in 1784*. He describes a four-o'clock dinner that he took in Torloisk, Mull, consisting of soup, black pudding, mutton, woodcock, and hot roast beef with 'cucumbers and ginger pickled in vinegar'. This was followed by cream with Madeira wine and a pudding made of barley meal, cream and currants and cooked in dripping. The latter I could probably do without but the roast beef and ginger cucumbers comes highly recommended.

Serves 8
4-rib of beef, weighing about 4.25kg/9½lb

For the salad:
1 large cucumber, coarsely grated (unpeeled)
100ml/3½fl oz white wine vinegar
1 heaped tablespoon granulated sugar
½ teaspoon salt
4–5cm/1½–2in piece of fresh root ginger, peeled and coarsely grated

Preheat the oven to 230°C/450°F/Gas 8. Ensure the beef is at room temperature, not straight from the fridge. Season it all over, then place it in a roasting tin (without any extra fat) and roast for 15 minutes. Reduce the oven temperature to 170°C/325°F/Gas 3 and cook for a further 17 minutes per 450g/1lb. This will result in medium-rare meat.

For the salad, combine all the ingredients, then leave for an hour or so before serving.

Once the meat is cooked to your liking, remove from the oven and leave to rest for at least 15 minutes. Then carve and serve with the salad and some roast potatoes and green vegetables.

Steak with Claret and Anchovies

Inspired by a recipe in Mistress Margaret Dods' *Manual*, this quick dish is simplicity itself. In her 1829 book she recommended frying the steaks for 12–15 minutes but I think that is too long – even if you like them well-done rather than rare.

Claret was commonly drunk with food and sometimes used in the kitchen because of the Auld Alliance links between the Bordeaux region of France and the port of Leith. In Dorothy Wordsworth's *Recollections of a Tour Made of Scotland in 1803*, she describes a stay in a house in the Highlands. The lady of the house 'set before me red and white wine, with the remnant of a loaf of wheaten bread which she took out of a cupboard in the sitting-room, and some delicious butter'. I find this description both charming and enlightening, as it demonstrates that not only were the men claret consumers but the women were, too. And what better accompaniment to wine than a good loaf of bread?

Serves 4

4 sirloin or rib-eye steaks

25g/1oz butter

4 anchovy fillets, snipped

1 rounded teaspoon Dijon mustard

150ml/5fl oz red wine

Bring the steaks to room temperature, then season them while you heat a large frying pan (or use 2 smaller pans) until very hot. Add the butter, then once it has melted add the steaks. Fry for 2–3 minutes on each side, only turning after 2 minutes, to allow a good crust to form.

Transfer the steaks to a warm plate. Add the anchovies, mustard and wine to the pan and let them bubble away for about 3 minutes, until reduced. Season with pepper (no salt, since the anchovies are salty). Serve the steaks with the sauce – and perhaps some sautéed potatoes and spinach.

Gigot of Lamb
with Turnip and Caper Sauce

In traditional recipes for gigot (leg) of mutton, the meat is boiled with carrots and turnips and then served with caper sauce. Since few cooks use mutton in the kitchen now (delicious though it is), I have adapted the idea to give a recipe for roast leg of lamb with roasted turnip (swede), accompanied by a piquant caper sauce. Serve with roast potatoes and green vegetables such as spinach and broccoli.

Serves 6
1.8kg/4lb leg of lamb
25g/1oz butter, softened
1 turnip (called swede in England), about 600g/1¼lb peeled weight
2 tablespoons olive oil
1 tablespoon mushroom ketchup or soy sauce

For the caper sauce:
40g/1½oz butter
40g/1½oz plain flour
300ml/10fl oz lamb stock
300ml/10fl oz full-fat milk
3 heaped tablespoons drained capers

Preheat the oven to 190°C/375°F/Gas 5. Place the lamb in a roasting tin and smear the butter over it. Season well with salt and pepper. Peel the turnip and chop it into bite-sized chunks. Place these around the meat and drizzle them with the oil, then season well. Roast the lamb for 1 hour, then drizzle the mushroom ketchup or soy sauce over the turnip chunks. Return to the oven until done to your liking – about 20 minutes. Remove and allow to rest while you make the caper sauce.

Melt the butter in a saucepan, add the flour and stir well. Gradually add the stock, then the milk, whisking constantly until smooth. Cook for a couple of minutes, then stir in the capers. Season with salt and pepper to taste. Serve with the lamb and turnip.

Roast Bubbly-jock
stuffed with Oysters

Bubbly-jock – the Scots name for turkey – became a Christmas treat in Scotland only relatively recently. The New Year has always been the more important festival.

I love to stuff turkey with oysters, which was common in the big Scottish houses in those halcyon days when oysters were not regarded as a luxury. Old-fashioned stuffing recipes were based on a mixture of breadcrumbs, parsley, lemon, lemon thyme, suet and eggs. Mine omits the suet and is light, fresh and absolutely delicious.

Be sure to stuff the turkey just before cooking, because of the raw oysters. If you cannot find a small turkey, use an extra large chicken instead. The giblets can be boiled up with a carrot, onion, bay leaf and a few peppercorns to make a stock for the gravy.

Serves 6

2.2–2.5kg/5lb–5lb 9oz free-range turkey, giblets removed

2 tablespoons olive oil

plain flour

a little oyster sauce (optional)

For the stuffing:

8 oysters, shucked (see page 65) but still in their shells, so you don't lose any of the juices

grated zest of 2 lemons

150g/5oz fresh breadcrumbs

20g/¾oz parsley, chopped

2 large free-range eggs

Preheat the oven to 220°C/425°F/Gas 7. For the stuffing, slice each oyster into 2–3 pieces and put them in a bowl, adding any precious juice from the shells. Mix in all the remaining stuffing ingredients and season well with salt and pepper.

Place the turkey in a roasting tin. Put some of the stuffing in the neck end (don't fill it too tightly) and some into the body cavity. Rub the oil all over the bird and season with salt and pepper. Cover loosely with oiled foil and roast for 20 minutes. Reduce the oven temperature to 190°C/375°F/Gas 5 and continue to cook for 1 hour, then remove the foil and cook until done – another 40 minutes or so. Test by inserting a sharp knife or skewer into the thickest part of the flesh: the juices should run clear.

Transfer the turkey to a carving dish and leave to rest for 10–15 minutes. Meanwhile, make a gravy: put the roasting tin on the hob over a medium heat and stir a heaped tablespoon of flour into the pan juices (pour some away first if there is too much fat). Cook for a couple of minutes, then gradually stir in the giblet stock and bring to the boil, whisking constantly until smooth. Season to taste. I also like to add a splash of oyster sauce to enhance the oyster flavour.

Roast Hebridean Lamb
with Skirlie Stuffing

The idea for this delicious dish comes from Linda Wood, who runs Leachin House, a guesthouse in Tarbert, Harris. She always buys her lamb from Charles Macleod in Stornoway — 1 hour north in Lewis — and cooks it for guests, sometimes in the French style with garlic and rosemary but sometimes with skirlie. She marinates the meat first in a mixture of fresh thyme, soy sauce and olive oil. I prefer simply to rub it inside and out with good olive oil, then stuff it with the cooled, freshly cooked skirlie. Remember to ask the butcher for the bone once he has tunnel-boned the lamb, so you can make stock for the gravy. I just boil the bones up with 2 fresh bay leaves, half an onion and cold water to cover.

   The lamb from the Stornoway butcher is from older animals than we might use on the mainland but the flavour is incomparable. The meat is from black-face and Cheviot lambs, from 6 to 15 months old. It goes without saying that Hebridean lambs are not intensively reared!

Serves 8
1 leg of lamb, weighing about 2.2kg/5lb, tunnel-boned (it should weigh about 1.8kg/4lb after boning)
olive oil
1 quantity of Skirlie (see page 113)
plain flour
lamb stock (see above)
a little red wine

Rub the meat inside and out with olive oil and leave somewhere cool for a few hours.

Preheat the oven to 220°C/425°F/Gas 7. Allow the skirlie to cool, then use it to stuff the lamb, taking care to pack it in neatly. Reshape the meat around it again and either tie it with string or simply tuck it into a tight-fitting roasting tin so it keeps its shape. Season all over with salt and pepper. Roast for 20 minutes, then reduce the oven temperature to 190°C/375°F/Gas 5 and roast for a further hour or so, until it is medium to well done, not rare.

Transfer the lamb to a serving platter and leave to rest for about 15 minutes before carving and serving with the skirlie. Meanwhile, make a simple gravy: put the roasting pan on top of the stove and stir about a heaped tablespoon of flour into the pan juices (pour some away first if there is too much fat). Gradually stir in the stock you have made from the bones and bring to the boil, whisking constantly. Add a splash of red wine and plenty of seasoning before serving.

Collops in the Pan

Undoubtedly another link with the Auld Alliance, the word collop, meaning a thin slice of meat (usually beef, venison or veal), is derived from the French *escalope*, which, according to *Larousse Gastronomique*, is 'slices of meat or fish of any kind, flattened slightly and fried in butter or some other fat'.

In old recipes, collops in the pan takes no more than 10 minutes to cook. I prefer to brown the onions well before adding the beef but it is still no longer than some 20 minutes from start to finish. Sometimes oyster pickle or walnut catsup was added to flavour it. I suggest using either mushroom ketchup (I think oriental oyster sauce would be inappropriate here) or Worcestershire sauce if you cannot find old-fashioned walnut catsup, or ketchup. Serve with mashed potatoes and a green vegetable.

Serves 4–6
50g/2oz butter
2 medium onions, peeled and sliced into rings
4 thin slices of rump steak, weighing about 1.1kg/2½lb in total
about 2 tablespoons mushroom ketchup, or Worcestershire sauce to taste

Heat the butter in a large frying pan (or 2 medium ones) and gently fry the onions for 10–15 minutes, until golden brown. Transfer to a plate with a slotted spoon. Increase the heat to high.

Cut the beef slices in half so you have 8 thin steaks. Season these and add to the pan. Cook for 4–5 minutes, turning once, until just done. Do not overcook.

Lower the heat, return the onions to the pan and add the mushroom ketchup or Worcestershire sauce. Stir and taste for seasoning, adding more ketchup or sauce if necessary. After a couple of minutes it should be ready to serve.

Haggis, Neeps and Tatties

Macsween of Edinburgh is famous worldwide for its haggis. From Hong Kong to Helsinki, its haggis (warm-reekin', rich, as Burns described it) has been consumed – no doubt with much whisky – anywhere and everywhere. Burns Night is, of course, the main time for haggis consumption but, according to marketing manager Jo Macsween, it is also popular throughout the year and is even served as a main course at weddings.

At Macsween's factory just outside Edinburgh, I watched the lamb lobes (lights) – which are the lungs – being cooked for some 3 hours, before being mixed with cooked beef fat, medium and pinhead oatmeal, onions and the special seasoning, which contains white pepper, mace, salt and coriander. After it has all been minced together, one of the Macsween family tastes it to check that the seasoning is correct. Then the mixture is used to fill the natural casings – ox bung or lamb's runner (intestine) that has been washed and salted. Then they are pricked and clipped at intervals, to allow for expansion, and cooked in the steam room for an hour or so before being left to cool overnight and vacuum packed. Because they are already cooked they only require reheating once you get them home. Typically they are served with neeps and tatties – and probably a wee dram. Or two.

The origins of the haggis are not set in stone. Although there are records of a similar 'sausage' in Greek writings, according to food historian Clarissa Dickson Wright the origins are more likely to be Scandinavian – a legacy of the Viking raids. The etymology supports this – the 'hag' part is linked to the Icelandic 'hoggva' and 'haggw', meaning 'to hew'.

However shrouded in mystery the history of the haggis may be, there is no disputing the fact that Robert Burns brought it into the limelight through his poetry in the eighteenth century. Before Burns it had been a homely, peasant dish. After his glorious poem, 'To a Haggis', it was – and is – 'Chieftan o' the Puddin'-race'.

Serves 4–6

1 haggis (the size depends on whether your guests are committed haggis eaters)
Bashed Neeps (see page 112) and Champit Tatties (see page 112), to serve

Preheat the oven to 180°C/350°F/Gas 4. Wrap the haggis in foil and heat it in the oven for about 45 minutes per 450g/1lb. Cut open the haggis and eat piping hot with neeps and tatties.

Stoved Howtowdie wi' Drappit Eggs

This delicious recipe is based on one in Meg Dods' 1829 *Manual* and is most definitely in the French style – the word stoved comes from the French *étuver*, which means to stew or heat in a stove. The chicken is browned all over, then stewed or cooked in the oven in stock until meltingly tender. Then some eggs are poached or dropped ('drappit') in the stock and these are served on spinach. A thin gravy is made with the stock once the eggs are done.

In my *Scots Thesaurus*, howtowdie is defined as 'a large young chicken for the pot, a young hen which has not begun to lay'. Some believe it comes from the Old French word *hutaudeau*, meaning a pullet. However, my former university lecturer, Dr Adamson, concluded that the derivation was in fact *hétoudeau* or *hétourdeau*, meaning capon, which seems more likely.

Be sure to use a free-range or organic chicken, whose flavour and texture will withstand long cooking better.

Serves 4

1 free-range chicken, weighing about 1.6–1.8kg/3½–4lb, giblets removed
1 white (mealie) pudding, skinned
75g/3oz butter
300g/10½oz shallots, peeled but left whole
700ml/1¼ pints hot light chicken stock
4 medium free-range eggs
300g/10½oz fresh spinach, washed and lightly cooked
1 heaped tablespoon cornflour

Preheat the oven to 180°C/350°F/Gas 4. Stuff the chicken with the white pudding. Heat the butter in a large flameproof casserole, then add the chicken and brown well all over. Tuck the shallots around it, pour over the hot stock and season well. Cover tightly with a lid (if it is not a good seal, use foil and a lid), transfer to the oven and cook for 1¼–1½ hours, until tender. Transfer the chicken and shallots to a large ashet (platter) and keep warm. Surround with the cooked spinach.

Place the casserole on the hob then, once the liquid is gently simmering, carefully drop in the eggs, one at a time, to poach (I like to draw the white gently around the yolk with a slotted spoon as they poach). After a couple of minutes, carefully remove the eggs with the slotted spoon and place on top of the spinach.

Mix the cornflour with 2 tablespoons of cold water and whisk this into the simmering stock. Cook for 5–10 minutes, whisking, until slightly thickened, then check the seasoning. Serve in a jug with the chicken.

6
game

At any time throughout the winter months, my butcher and game dealer has pheasant, roe deer, teal, widgeon, partridge, hare and rabbit, all of which are lean, flavoursome and healthy. They are also some of the most natural produce available, free from additives, hormones or chemical feed. And because they are wild, they have to work hard to obtain their food and so have very little fat on them. With our minds set firmly on reducing our fat intake these days, surely game constitutes an ideal modern food.

Although game was originally eaten by everyone (prehistoric man's diet was not all roots and berries), it gradually became exclusive to the privileged, and remained so until relatively recently. Images of massive haunches of venison served on large ashets with pomp and ceremony suggest baronial splendour – the landed gentry rather than Scotland's 'ordinary' folk. Grouse has definitely become a luxury item, mainly because of the ridiculous price on August 12th (when it should never be eaten, as it has not been hung). But although it is always fairly dear, later in the season prices come down and older, cheaper grouse can be used to make superb casseroles and terrines. Venison has also become less expensive, as it is now farmed. Provided you buy from a reputable supplier, farmed venison is excellent, and has the advantage of being available all year. If, however, you can buy some wild venison in season, such as fillet of roe deer, then do so, for a truly memorable treat.

This chapter contains some simple recipes using Scotland's game. Many are interchangeable, depending on availability. But with all the recipes, bear in mind that game is lean and so if you are roasting it, overcooking will ruin what should be a splendid feast. Casseroling and making pies or crumbles is a less unforgiving way of preparing it. Both ought to be tried, however, for game is one of the few culinary treats that have not been ruined by intensive production methods. It is a healthy food that deserves more acclaim.

Rabbit Pie

Rabbit used to be very popular cooked in stews and casseroles as a change from mince, or sometimes made into pies. This pie was inspired by a traditional 'Kingdom of Fife Pie' – rabbit joints and forcemeat balls tucked under a puff pastry crust and baked. I am not keen on meat still on the bone under pastry, so I cook the rabbit in advance and remove the meat from the bones. I also miss out the forcemeat, but keep in the characteristic sliced hard-boiled eggs. Eat this with mashed potatoes and a green vegetable or two.

Serves 4
1 plump rabbit, cleaned and jointed
1 heaped tablespoon flour, seasoned with salt and pepper
50g/2oz butter
110g/4oz smoked streaky bacon, chopped
1 onion, peeled and chopped
1 large leek, sliced
400ml/14fl oz hot chicken stock
3 thick sprigs of thyme
2 large free-range eggs, hard-boiled and sliced
250g/9oz ready-rolled puff pastry
beaten egg, to glaze

My butcher always advises rubbing wild rabbit with salt then rinsing well under a cold running tap, but if it is a farmed rabbit you probably will not need to do this.

Coat the rabbit joints in the flour, then fry in half the butter until browned all over. Transfer to a plate. Heat the remaining butter in the pan and gently fry the bacon, onion and leek for 10 minutes or so, until soft. Return the rabbit to the pan and stir in the hot stock. Add the thyme and some seasoning, bring to the boil, then cover and simmer over a low heat for 1 hour, until the rabbit is tender. Check the seasoning again while it is still hot, then leave to cool – I leave it overnight.

The next day, scrape off any surface fat and remove the rabbit joints. Take off all the meat and place in a 1.5 litre/2½ pint pie dish with the bacon and enough of the stock just to cover the meat. Top with the sliced hard-boiled eggs.

Preheat the oven to 220°C/425°F/Gas 7. Cut a long strip off the rolled-out pastry. Wet the edges of the pie dish and press the strip of pastry all around. Wet this and place the remaining pastry over the top. Press the edges to seal and then trim off any excess. Crimp the edges with your thumb and forefinger, then brush all over with beaten egg. Snip a couple of holes in the centre, then bake the pie for about 30 minutes, until puffed up and golden brown. Cover loosely with foil for the last 5–10 minutes if necessary, to prevent burning.

Serve at once.

Wild Duck with Juniper Sauce
and Glazed Shallots

This recipe is from Rosemary Shrager, chef at Amhuinnsuidhe Castle on the North Harris Estate in the Outer Hebrides. She uses duck from South Uist, south of Harris.

Serves 6
3 wild duck
extra virgin olive oil
a few sprigs of thyme
1 onion, peeled and chopped
20 shallots, peeled
but left whole
3 celery sticks, chopped
2 garlic cloves, peeled and
chopped
1 heaped tablespoon raisins
110g/4oz unsalted butter

For the sauce:
50g/2oz butter, plus a knob
2 bacon rashers, chopped
1 leek, chopped
600ml/1 pint red wine
600ml/1 pint chicken stock
1 tablespoon redcurrant or
bramble jelly
12 juniper berries, crushed

Remove the legs and breasts from the ducks and marinate these for 4 hours in a little olive oil with most of the thyme and some salt and pepper. Preheat the oven to 190°C/375°F/Gas 5.

Put the duck carcasses in a roasting tin (breaking them up if large), add the onion and roast for 20 minutes, until brown, then remove.

Place the shallots, celery and garlic in an ovenproof dish lined with a large piece of foil. Add the raisins and a little thyme and dot with the butter. Seal the foil and put into the oven for up to 1 hour, until tender.

Meanwhile, make the sauce: melt 50g/2oz of the butter in a medium saucepan and gently fry the bacon and leek in it for 5 minutes. Add the wine and boil until reduced by half. Add the chicken stock with the roasted duck bones and boil until the liquid is reduced to one third. Remove the bones, then add the jelly and juniper berries. Simmer until the sauce is reduced to about 225ml/8fl oz. Strain into a clean pan.

Heat a little olive oil in a large frying pan, add the duck pieces and seal quickly on both sides. Place in an ovenproof dish and roast (same oven temperature as the carcasses) for 8–10 minutes, depending on thickness – the legs will take a little longer than this. Remove and leave to rest for 5 minutes before serving.

To finish the sauce, reheat if necessary, whisk in the knob of butter, then check the seasoning. To serve, place a pile of the shallot and celery mixture in the middle of each serving plate. Slice the meat from the duck breasts and legs and place it on top, surrounding it with the sauce.

Pheasant and Lovage Crumble

Because of its dietary habits – it does not generally eat high moorland heather – pheasant has a much milder flavour than other game such as grouse. Indeed, some supermarket pheasant can taste rather like free-range chicken or turkey. Presuming your butcher hangs his pheasant well, however, the meat should be nicely – if not overtly – gamy. My game butcher, Alec Smith at George Bower, lets me know when it is time to sell 'old grouse' (casserole birds) cheaply, which means the pheasant season is nigh. The season lasts from 1 October to 1 February.

Lovage is an old-fashioned herb that was widely used in Scotland in the past and still grows in many people's gardens. If you cannot get hold of it, however, use parsley instead.

Serves 8
3 medium oven-ready pheasant
300ml/10fl oz chicken or pheasant stock
300ml/10fl oz dry cider
2 bay leaves
a handful of lovage stalks (use the leaves for the crumble topping)
50g/2oz butter
200g/7oz streaky bacon, chopped
1 large onion, peeled and chopped
4 celery sticks, chopped
200g/7oz button mushrooms
50g/2oz plain flour
150g/5oz whole cooked chestnuts
(I use vacuum-packed)

For the crumble topping:
50g/2oz porridge oats
150g/5oz plain flour
1 heaped tablespoon
chopped lovage leaves
50g/2oz hazelnuts, chopped
125g/4½oz butter, diced

Place the pheasant in a large pan with the stock, cider, bay leaves and lovage stalks. Bring slowly to the boil, then cover and simmer for 45–50 minutes, until the birds are just cooked. Remove from the heat and leave to cool, then strain, reserving the stock. Remove the meat from the pheasants and cut into large chunks. Heat the butter in a pan, add the bacon, onion, celery and the whole mushrooms and fry for about 10 minutes. Add the flour and cook, stirring constantly, for 1 minute. Then add the chestnuts and gradually pour in the reserved stock. Simmer over a medium heat for 3–4 minutes until thick, stirring constantly. Season to taste with salt and pepper and add the meat. Tip into a large gratin dish and leave to cool.

Preheat the oven to 180°C/350°F/Gas 4. For the crumble, place the oats, flour, lovage and nuts in a bowl and rub in the butter. Sprinkle this over the cooled pheasant mixture, pressing it down gently, and bake for about 1 hour or until golden brown and bubbling. Serve with crusty bread and salad.

Roast Grouse with Blaeberries

Rather than buying grouse at the beginning of the season, when they are expensive and haven't been hung properly, it's best to wait until early September, then enjoy young grouse for the entire month until the older birds come in for casseroling.

This simple roast dish calls for grouse to be stuffed with a mixture of butter and blaeberries, covered with bacon to prevent them drying out, then roasted in a very hot oven. Blaeberries are what we Scots call bilberries. If you cannot find them, use cultivated blueberries instead. Serve with Skirlie (see page 113), roast potatoes and a green vegetable.

Serves 2
2 young oven-ready grouse
125g/4½oz blaeberries
50g/2oz butter, softened
6 back bacon rashers
1 tablespoon blaeberry jelly
(or bramble/blackberry jelly)
2 tablespoons red wine

Preheat the oven to 230°C/450°F/Gas 8. Wash out the insides of the grouse and dry well. Mix the berries into the butter (gently, so they do not burst) and season with salt and pepper. Stuff this into each body cavity. Lay the bacon on top, trying to cover all the breast. Place the birds in a small buttered roasting tin and roast for 20 minutes, then remove from the oven. Tip out the contents of the birds' cavities into the tin. Place the grouse on a serving dish to rest in a low oven (if you have only one oven, leave them in it with the door open) for at least 10 minutes, loosely covered with foil. Place the roasting tin over a direct heat, add the jelly and wine and bubble away for 2–3 minutes, then season to taste. Pour the contents into a small sauceboat and serve with the grouse.

Game Loaf

This recipe was inspired by one in Elizabeth Craig's 1965 book, *What's Cooking in Scotland?*, which calls for young grouse breasts to be tucked inside a sandwich loaf with mushrooms and bacon, then covered in a rich game sauce and baked in the oven. I have developed her recipe – which is rather rich – to make a loaf that is lighter and more up-to-date. It is basically a variation on the famous shooter's sandwich, which is made with rump steak. This version is good to take on picnics or just for a simple winter lunch, perhaps after a warming bowl of soup.

I buy pheasant breasts from my butcher but if you can't, simply remove them from the bird (pheasant or grouse) by carefully running a sharp knife as close to the backbone as possible.

Serves 4-6
1 sandwich loaf,
weighing about 750g/1lb 10oz
4 tablespoons olive oil
6 pheasant breasts
or 6-8 grouse breasts
300g/10½oz large mushrooms,
thickly sliced
1 tablespoon thyme leaves

Cut one end off the loaf and set aside. Carefully remove much of the centre crumb, ensuring you leave a thickish crust – about 4cm/1½ inches all round. Heat half the oil in a large frying pan and add the game breasts. Season well and fry all over for 8–10 minutes, until just done. Tuck the breasts inside the loaf to form the first layer.

Add the remaining oil to the pan and fry the mushrooms for about 10 minutes, then add the thyme and plenty of salt and pepper. Tuck the mushrooms on top of the game and drizzle in all the pan juices. Replace the end of the bread, wrap the loaf in a double sheet of foil and leave in the fridge overnight, well weighted down (I use 2 orange juice cartons). The next day, remove the foil and cut the loaf into thick slices.

Roast Partridge

with Chanterelles

There are many elaborate recipes for partridge in old Scottish recipe books, from soups to soufflés. Because partridge is rather more of a treat nowadays – and expensive, too – I tend only to roast this fine bird, sometimes wrapped in bacon, sometimes stuffed with grapes. But I like to keep it simple.

If you can find fresh chanterelles, substitute about 150g/5oz for the dried ones, omitting the soaking.

Serves 2

20g/¾ oz dried chanterelles
100ml/3½fl oz dry white wine
2 tablespoons olive oil
2 oven-ready partridge
2 garlic cloves, peeled and chopped
½ small onion, peeled and finely chopped
1 heaped teaspoon plain flour
2 tablespoons double cream
a dash of truffle oil

Rinse the mushrooms and soak them in the wine for an hour or so.

Preheat the oven to 230°C/450°F/Gas 8. Heat half the oil in a small roasting tin on top of the hob, add the partridge and brown them all over. Season well, then transfer to the oven and roast for 5 minutes. Reduce the oven temperature to 200°C/400°F/Gas 6 and roast for a further 12–15 minutes, basting once. Test by inserting a skewer into the thickest part of the flesh; the juices should run clear or very slightly pink. Remove from the oven and leave to rest, loosely covered with foil, for at least 10 minutes.

Heat the remaining oil in a small saucepan and gently fry the garlic and onion in it for 5 minutes. Drain the mushrooms, reserving the liquid, and add them to the pan. Fry for 5–10 minutes, until tender, then increase the heat. Sprinkle in the flour and cook for 1 minute, stirring. Add the reserved wine and the cream. Simmer for 3–5 minutes, then season to taste with salt and pepper and a dash of truffle oil.

Serve the birds with the chanterelle sauce and either sautéed potatoes or tagliatelle and a green vegetable such as spinach or broccoli.

Roast Venison
with Blackcurrant Sauce

In the past, venison often appeared on the menus of the many inns for travellers throughout the Highlands, although it was perhaps not always treated with the greatest of respect. Writer Thomas Pennant, visiting Kinlochleven in the late 1700s, wrote, 'Breakfast on most excellent minced stag, the only form I thought that animal good in.'

This recipe makes rather more fitting use of venison, and is a splendid Sunday lunch alternative to beef or lamb. If you are using wild venison, it might be a good idea to marinate it first to ensure tenderness. In the Georgian period, venison was often marinated for many hours in a mixture of claret, vinegar and lemon juice, then the marinade was used to baste the haunch as it roasted. The original recipe for this was said to have been invented by the chefs of Mary of Guise.

If you cannot be bothered to make the sauce (though it's very easy), then serve the venison simply with a pot of blackcurrant or rowan jelly, a bowl of steamed new potatoes and some green vegetables.

Serves 6–8
50g/2oz butter
3 teaspoons blackcurrant jelly
1.3–1.8kg/3–4lb haunch (or saddle) of venison on the bone
3 tablespoons red wine
2 teaspoons blackcurrant (or raspberry) vinegar
300ml/10fl oz hot game or beef stock
3–4 sprigs of thyme
a handful of fresh blackcurrants

Preheat the oven to 230°C/425°F/Gas 8. Melt the butter and 2 teaspoons of the blackcurrant jelly in a large frying pan. Once sizzling, add the meat and brown it all over, then transfer it to a roasting tin, pouring all the butter over it. Season well with salt and pepper. Place in the oven and cook for 12–15 minutes per 450g/1lb – 12 minutes for rare, 15 for medium-rare; because it is such a lean meat, venison should not be cooked beyond medium. Then place the meat on a carving board, cover with a double sheet of foil (or place, uncovered, in a plate-warming oven) and leave to rest for about 20 minutes.

Meanwhile, make the sauce: pour off most of the fat from the roasting tin, leaving in only a teaspoon or so, then put the tin on the hob. Add the wine and vinegar and stir to scrape up all the bits from the base of the tin. Boil for a couple of minutes, then add the hot stock, the remaining teaspoon of jelly and the thyme and simmer for 4–5 minutes, stirring, until reduced to a sauce-like consistency. Season to taste, then sieve into a warmed serving dish or jug. Add the blackcurrants, stirring gently to heat them through.

Carve the venison into slices and serve with the blackcurrant sauce.

7

vegetables and grains

Whereas Scots have always been masters of the soup pot and mistresses of the rolling pin, vegetables have never quite been our thing. Apart from potatoes, turnips, kail, leeks, onions and carrots, they have never taken pride of place at the table. Unless, of course, they were in the soup pot. Depending on the season, some other vegetables, such as peas, cabbages and Brussels sprouts, were also eaten, but as a general rule everyday fare was root vegetables with an onion thrown in for flavour. Other vegetables were so simply cooked that they merit no recipe. I remember my sister and I picking from the long rows of peas in the garden. These would then be podded, boiled and served with nothing other than a good 'dod' of butter. I also remember my father thinning out his lettuces and pulling up some spring onions (often known in Scotland as 'sybies') for a fresh summer salad with cold meat, beetroot and tomato.

The few old-fashioned recipes for vegetables are much of a muchness. Colcannon and kailkenny are Highland and north-eastern variations of a potato and cabbage mash, with additions such as cream or turnip (swede). Clapshot and rumbledethumps are Orcadian and Borders versions of a mash of potatoes and turnip or cabbage, with the Borders dish being topped with grated cheese and baked in the oven. Stovies are sliced potatoes slowly cooked with onion in dripping and meat juices until soft and tender. Champit tatties are mashed potatoes, while bashed neeps are mashed turnips (swede).

There has, therefore, been little variety in traditional Scottish vegetables when served on their own. With our one-pot cooking ethos (the kail-pot over the peat fire) we tended to throw vegetables straight from the garden or kail-yard into a pot for stew or soup, thereby retaining all their goodness – there was method in our madness. And when we did come to cook vegetables separately, they were – and still are – of the finest quality, with a wonderful flavour. Simple, homely and delicious – Scotland's vegetables on a plate.

Stovies

This is a delicious dish of onions and potatoes fried in dripping (you can use the white fat on the surface of the meat jelly after pouring off the meat juices from your roasting tin and chilling), then cooked slowly in the meat jelly (or stock) until tender. Stovies are very similar to pan haggerty, a dish from the north-east of England consisting of sliced onions and potatoes cooked slowly in dripping in a deep covered frying pan. Just like stovies, this was traditionally served on Mondays after a Sunday roast.

Stovies are now classic pub fare throughout Scotland – understandably, since they are ideal for soaking up vast quantities of alcohol. They vary from region to region. In Arbroath and Aberdeen, corned beef or chopped roast meat is often added and they are served with oatcakes. In Orkney, pieces of brisket are stirred in.

Customers at my Edinburgh butcher's crumble Lorne sausage on top of the stovies as they cook, on the recommendation of the butcher's daughter, Audrey. However, they already have so much flavour from the dripping and meat jelly that I like them best served plain, with thick oatcakes and a glass of cold milk.

Serves 3–4
2 heaped tablespoons dripping
(use butter if you have no dripping)
2 onions, peeled and sliced
750g/1lb 10oz potatoes, peeled
and thinly sliced
2 tablespoons meat jelly (or beef stock)

Melt the dripping in a large heavy saucepan, add the onions and fry for 10–15 minutes, until golden. Add the potato slices and turn carefully in the fat: be careful the slices do not break up. Season well with salt and pepper, then add the meat jelly and heat until melted. Cover tightly and cook over a low heat for about 40 minutes or until the potatoes are tender and have absorbed all the liquid. Add a splash of hot water if they seem too dry. While they cook, shake the pan often to prevent sticking; do not stir or you will break up the delicate potato slices. Serve piping hot.

Clapshot

This dish from Orkney is similar to Northern Ireland's champ and also to colcannon, which is found in southern Ireland and the Highlands of Scotland. Clapshot differs by having turnips – called swede in England and, for short, neeps in Scotland – mixed with the potatoes instead of cabbage, spring onions or leeks. Because neeps and tatties are typical accompaniments to haggis, I suggest serving a dish of clapshot to ring the changes.

It also makes a very comforting vegetarian dish (if you use butter, not dripping), served in warm bowls with thick oatcakes and a glass of cold milk or buttermilk.

Serves 4–6
500g/1lb 2oz (peeled weight) potatoes, peeled and cut up
500g/1lb 2oz (peeled weight) turnip (swede), peeled and cut up
50g/2oz butter or dripping
1–2 tablespoons chopped chives

Put the vegetables in a pan of cold salted water, then cover and bring to the boil. Simmer for 15–20 minutes, depending on size, until tender, then drain. Return them to the pan, cover and shake the pan over a very low heat to dry them off completely. Remember, turnips are rather watery so unless you dry them off well the mixture will be sloppy.

Mash the vegetables with the butter or dripping, then add salt and pepper to taste and stir in the chives. Serve piping hot.

Grilled Dulse

Another idea from Margaret Horn of Auchmithie's But 'n' Ben. Dulse used to be a well-known snack in local pubs, roasted or grilled and served with a splash of vinegar. Given the innate saltiness of any seaweed, this was a fairly canny way of increasing thirst levels in the pub goer! The traditional way to grill dulse would have been to cook with a red-hot poker over the embers of a peat fire until it turned green.

Grilled dulse can be served with drinks instead of nuts or olives but it is also good as an unusual garnish on soups or pasta, or tossed over salads at the last minute. On the Isle of Barra, it was often eaten as a relish with potatoes.

When picking any wild seaweed, be sure it is from unpolluted water.

Serves 4
a large handful of freshly picked dulse, well washed
malt vinegar

Place the dulse under a hot grill for about 4–5 minutes, by which time it should be green and crisp (watch it like a hawk; it burns very quickly). Sprinkle with a little vinegar and eat hot or cold, but do not refrigerate.

Champit Tatties

Traditionally served with bashed neeps and haggis at a Burns Supper, this is Scotland's answer to the increasingly fashionable mash. You can flavour it with chopped spring onions, parsley or chives, adorn with crisp fried onion or bacon pieces, or sprinkle each mound with a fine mantle of Skirlie (see page 113) for a good contrasting crunch.

Serves 4–6
1kg/2¼lb floury potatoes
(e.g. King Edward, Fianna or Maris Piper),
peeled and chopped
100g/3½oz butter
100ml/3½fl oz hot full-fat milk

Cook the potatoes in boiling salted water until tender. Drain well and return to the pan over a low heat until thoroughly dry. Once dry, add the butter and mash with a potato masher, then add the hot milk and mash again, tasting and adding salt and pepper accordingly. Serve piping hot.

Bashed Neeps

Together with champit tatties, this is the traditional accompaniment to haggis. It is also good served with any roast meat or with grilled sausages. Although I suggest adding some nutmeg, Meg Dodds recommended a little powdered ginger in her mashed turnips, to help 'correct the flatulent properties of this esculent'!

What we in Scotland call neeps is actually short for turnip – which is in fact not what is called turnip down south but swede. I realise it is not everyone's favourite vegetable but I love it. A dish of piping hot, buttery bashed neeps is my idea of bliss.

Serves 4–6
750g/1lb 10oz turnip
(called swede in England),
peeled and cut into chunks
50g/2oz butter
freshly grated nutmeg

Cook the turnip in boiling salted water for about 20 minutes, until tender. Drain, then return to the saucepan and place over a low heat, shaking the pan often, to dry out completely.

Using a potato masher, mash the turnip with the butter, then add salt, pepper and grated nutmeg to taste. Serve piping hot.

Skirlie

Skirlie has the same ingredients as mealie puddings but is fried. The name derives from 'skirl in the pan' – the hissing noise it makes while frying, as in 'the skirl of the pipes'. In Aberdeenshire skirlie is traditionally served on a Saturday with champit (mashed) tatties. In other areas it is served as an accompaniment to mince but is also excellent as a stuffing for chicken, game or lamb. And I far prefer it with roast game birds to the more usual fried breadcrumbs. But perhaps that is purely national prejudice.

Most recipes recommend using medium oatmeal but sometimes coarse (half medium, half pinhead) is used, which gives a rougher, nuttier texture.

Serves 4–6
50g/2oz dripping or suet (or 25g/1oz butter and 2 tablespoons olive oil)
1 medium onion, peeled and finely chopped
100g/3½oz medium or coarse oatmeal

Melt the fat in a pan. Add the onion and cook slowly for at least 10 minutes, until softened and golden brown. Then add the oatmeal, stirring until the fat is absorbed. You might be able to add a little more oatmeal. Cook over a medium heat, stirring often, until it is toasted and crumbly – about 8–10 minutes.

Season to taste with salt and pepper. Serve piping hot, or leave to cool and use as a stuffing.

Big Peas and Lang Tatties

Big peas and lang tatties. Could there be a more evocative name for a dish? According to food writer Grace Mulligan, it was the name given to the portions of marrowfat peas and chips bought in the Overgate, in the centre of Dundee, for many years, certainly until the mid 1930s. My parents knew this as a 'Buster': chips and Buster (marrowfat) peas. For 1d (one old penny) you were given a deep, old-fashioned saucer full of chips and big peas, which were sprinkled with vinegar, the only flavouring apart from salt. Unlike mushy peas, which are often cooked up with onion or bacon, Buster peas are cooked dried peas, plain and simple.

The lang tatties, or chips, were, according to Grace Mulligan, cut from the giant potatoes that the potato merchants separated from their harvest. They often had splits inside them which you could not detect from the outside, and they would have been cheaper to buy and easier to peel. The chips were always fried in an unspecified fat, which presumably was beef dripping.

Grace can remember being taken by her grandfather to the market in Dundee, where they sat on wooden benches inside a tent-like structure in the middle of the old Dundee tenements. This is where they had the Buster stalls. The vats of hot fat and peas were cooked over open fires in big iron boxes, rather like old-fashioned ranges. This was quite dangerous, with small customers sitting directly underneath huge vats of boiling fat and hot peas!

These days I serve big peas at home when I am treating the children to fish and chips, which, in my humble opinion, beats Indian or Chinese takeaways any day.

Serves 4
For the big peas:
300g/10½oz dried marrowfat peas, soaked overnight and then drained
vinegar (malt is traditional; wine vinegar is also fine)

For the lang tatties:
4 large floury potatoes (e.g. Maris Piper, Record, Pentland Dell or Fianna)
fat or oil for deep-frying

Put the soaked peas in a saucepan and pour over enough boiling water to cover generously – about 1 litre/1¾ pints. Bring to the boil and cook, covered, for about 1¼–1½ hours, until tender. Drain off any excess liquid if necessary, then season with plenty of salt and sprinkle with vinegar.

For the lang tatties, peel the potatoes and cut them into thick chips (not dainty french fries). Place in a bowl of cold water to remove excess starch, then drain and dry thoroughly. Half-fill a deep-fat fryer or large deep saucepan with fat or oil and heat to 180°C/350°F. If you have no thermometer, drop in a chip; it should sizzle in a mass of tiny bubbles. Cook the chips for 5–6 minutes, then remove from the pan and drain. Increase the temperature to 190°C/375°F (or when a tester chip turns golden brown in about 1 minute) and cook the chips for about 3 minutes, until golden brown and crisp. Drain well, then sprinkle liberally with salt. Serve with the big peas.

Rumbledethumps

This is a Borders dish of potatoes and cabbage, topped with cheese and browned in the oven. My recipe also includes turnip, as this is how my mother prepares it. The name is meant to come from 'rumbled' (mashed or stirred together) and 'thumped' (pounded together). Chopped chives or spring onions can also be added.

Serves 4

600g/1¼lb (peeled weight) potatoes, peeled and chopped

400g/14oz (peeled weight) turnip (called swede in England), peeled and chopped

250g/9oz cabbage, preferably Savoy, finely sliced

75g/3oz butter

25g/1oz mature Cheddar cheese, grated

Preheat the oven to 180°C/350°F/Gas 4. Put the potatoes and turnip in cold salted water, cover and bring to the boil. Simmer until tender, then drain. Return the vegetables to the pan, cover and shake the pan over a very low heat to dry them off completely. Heat 50g/2oz of the butter in a pan, add the cabbage and cook until just tender but still bright green. Tip the cabbage and its butter into the pan of potatoes and turnips with the remaining butter and mash together well. Season with salt and pepper to taste and transfer to an ovenproof dish. Top with the cheese, then cover and bake for 25–30 minutes, until golden brown and piping hot.

White (or Mealie) Puddings

Mealie pudding is one of many traditional foods that bring back memories for me – this time of Dundee University in the mid 1970s. Late at night a group of us would traipse down to Greasy Pete's or Sweaty Betty's for a white pudding supper. This was a 'dressed' mealie pudding and chips. The pudding was denuded of its skin, then dipped in batter and deep-fried until crisp and golden on the outside, soft and squishy inside. There are few better tastes and textures if a bout of late-night hunger hits and it is stodge your body needs. The deep-fried Mars bar had not been invented at that time, otherwise it would definitely have been an option.

But mealie puddings are not unhealthy. Made from oatmeal, suet and onions, they were prepared – along with black puddings – whenever beef cattle were killed. The intestines were cleaned, then filled with the oatmeal mixture before being tied up and boiled. In rural Aberdeenshire the mealie mixture was sometimes packed into a scalded cloth and tied, leaving room for the oatmeal to swell, then boiled in the same way. Eaten traditionally as an accompaniment to mince and tatties or stew, they are also sliced on top of mince in Aberdeenshire and heated through in the oven, so that they absorb the fat from the mince. They also make the most sublime stuffing for chicken, too.

The following recipe comes from my Auntie Bette's mother-in-law, Granny Henderson. She was a stalwart of the Kirk and used to make dozens of mealies for church sales. Since she was boiling many at a time, she used her large washtub to boil up the puddings. I am sure it gave the socks an interesting flavour.

Makes 6–8

pudding skins
(natural casings are available
from good butcher's)
900g/2lb medium oatmeal
2 onions, peeled and finely chopped
450g/1lb beef suet, shredded
Jamaica pepper (ground allspice)

Prepare the skins by soaking them in salted water overnight and then rinsing well in clear cold water. Toast the oatmeal lightly in a moderate oven or under the grill. Mix it with the onions, suet and some salt and Jamaica pepper to taste. Stuff the mixture into the skins – not too full, since the oatmeal will swell. Tie the ends in a knot to secure and drop the puddings into a large pan of boiling water. Cook steadily for 1 hour, pricking the skins occasionally to prevent bursting. Once cooked, they will keep well for several weeks – preferably stored in a tub of oatmeal. When required, heat through either in simmering water or in a medium oven for about 20 minutes, until piping hot.

8 hot and cold puddings

Puddings are very dear to all Scots' hearts. It's that confounded sweet tooth of ours, which means that unless we finish a meal with a good slab of cake or have a scone with our cup of tea, we will be more than ready for pudding. If there is none, there will be a big sulk. Or a quick drive to the nearest petrol station or corner shop to indulge in some chocolate or sweeties. We didn't get our bad dental records for nothing.

Nowadays, people are more concerned about their sugar and fat intake and so are eating fewer puddings. But every now and then it is wonderful – and truly therapeutic – to make a lovely old-fashioned pudding that will be enjoyed by the whole family, safe in the knowledge that if it is home-made it will be a lot more wholesome than any commercial product.

Some of the recipes in this chapter are classics – Scots trifle, cranachan, Atholl brose. What would a Burns Supper be without one of these traditional dishes to round off the haggis and whisky-based meal? Others, such as cloutie dumpling or treacle duff, meant a lot to me during my childhood. I remember watching cloutie dumpling being mixed and lovingly wrapped in its floury 'clout', then boiled away for hours as I hung around, becoming more and more ravenous, waiting for the dumpling to emerge, plump and glorious, from its steamy bath. And treacle duff, a dark, sticky steamed pudding served in a puddle of custard, was another of my all-time favourites.

Finally there are some modernised versions of extremely old recipes – sticky toffee pudding, oatmeal praline ice-cream, apple frushie. All of them are easy to make and, as long as you use the best ingredients, all are absolutely delicious. Try them and see.

Treacle Duff

This is basically a steamed pudding flavoured with black treacle and is inspired by recipes in various old cookery books from the Kirk Women's Guild or WI, dating from the early 1900s. Treacle duff is among the usual roly-poly, seven-cup and canary puddings, beside lesser-known ones such as Brown George pudding (with mixed spice), Aeroplane pudding (with jam) and Auchingoul pudding (with lemon). My treacle duff recipe is similar to one called Marina pudding, a black-treacle-based mixture, but with the addition of a cup of raisins. Add these if you wish; with or without, this dark, treacly pud is truly memorable.

Serves 6
175g/6oz self-raising flour, sifted
1 teaspoon ground ginger
a pinch of salt
110g/4oz unsalted butter, softened
100g/3½oz dark muscovado sugar
2 large free-range eggs
2 level tablespoons black treacle

Place everything in a bowl and beat with an electric mixer for about 3 minutes, until smooth. Then tip into a lightly buttered 1 litre/1¾ pint pudding basin. To cover, fold a pleat in a double sheet of buttered foil (to allow room for expansion) and tie it securely over the basin with string. I make a string handle by threading the string twice from one side to the other so it is easy to lift. Scrunch up the edges of the foil so it does not sit in the water. Place the basin in a large saucepan over a low heat and pour boiling water carefully down the sides to come about half way up the basin. The water should be simmering gently, not boiling furiously. Cover the pan tightly and steam for 1¾–2 hours, topping up the water level if necessary. Leave for 5 minutes, then remove the foil, run a knife around the edge of the pudding and invert it on to a warm serving plate. Serve with custard.

Steamed Marmalade Pudding

The better the marmalade you use, the more divine this pudding will be. Serve with a large jug of custard.

Serves 6
2 heaped tablespoons Dundee
marmalade
110g/4oz butter, softened
110g/4oz golden caster sugar
2 large free-range eggs
175g/6oz self-raising flour, sifted
grated zest of 1 small orange
2 tablespoons milk

Butter a 1 litre/1¾ pint pudding basin and place the marmalade in the base. Cream together the butter and sugar until light and fluffy, then beat in the eggs one at a time, adding a little of the flour with each egg. Using a metal spoon, fold in the remaining flour, the orange zest and milk. Once well combined, spoon the mixture carefully on top of the marmalade and smooth the top.

To cover, fold a pleat in a double sheet of buttered foil (to allow room for expansion) and tie it securely over the basin with string. I make a string handle by threading the string twice from one side to the other so it is easy to lift. Scrunch up the edges of the foil so it does not sit in the water.

Place the basin in a large saucepan over a low heat. Pour boiling water carefully down the sides to come about half way up the basin. The water should be simmering gently, not boiling furiously. Cover the pan tightly and steam for 1¾–2 hours, topping up the water level if necessary.

Remove the pudding from the pan, wait 5–10 minutes, then remove the foil, run a knife around the edge and carefully invert the pudding on to a warm serving plate.

Cloutie Dumpling

My Auntie Muriel has been making cloutie dumpling for family birthdays for as long as I can remember. She will tie on her pinnie and stir together the ingredients, which she always says she couldn't possibly write down, for she tells me there's a 'ticky of this and a ticky of that'. No one ever used to write cloutie dumpling recipes, they just made them. But I have managed to pin her down and the following recipe is the one made for the family by her or often by her housekeeper, Mrs Patullo, who was Austrian and whose apple strudel was better than any shopbought one.

The word cloth is the origin of this dumpling recipe, as cloot or clout is Scots for cloth. It refers to the cloth in which the dumpling is boiled. Unlike other dumplings or steamed puddings, it forms a characteristic 'skin', made by sprinkling flour and sugar into the cloth before filling it with the mixture. Beware clouties without skin, as they are not authentic. The skin must be dried off before serving and nowadays this is done in the oven. But my mother tells me her task as youngest child was to dry the dumpling in front of the open fireplace. She would sit there on a stool for 15–20 minutes, turning the dumpling round and round until it was dried off and ready to eat. Since it was made only for special occasions such as birthdays (in which case there were silver threepennies hidden inside, similar to charms in a Christmas pudding), this was a chore worth doing well. It would then be eaten with custard, but is now also served with cream or ice-cream. Next day any leftovers would be fried in rendered suet and eaten with bacon for breakfast.

If you want to add coins, wrap 5p pieces or charms in waxed or greaseproof paper and add to the mixture.

Serves 8

225g/8oz plain flour, sifted
200g/7oz golden caster sugar
1 level teaspoon ground cinnamon
1 heaped teaspoon mixed spice
110g/4oz shredded suet
110g/4oz sultanas
110g/4oz currants
110g/4oz stoned dates, finely chopped
1 heaped teaspoon bicarbonate of soda
about 200ml/7fl oz milk, sour milk or cold tea
flour and caster sugar, for sprinkling

Mix the first 9 ingredients together in a bowl with enough of the liquid to give the dough a stiff dropping consistency.

Dip a large pudding cloth or tea towel into boiling water, then drain well and lay out flat on a table. Sprinkle with flour and then sugar (I use my flour and sugar shakers): you need an even, but not thick, layer. Place the mixture in the middle of the cloth, then bring the ends up and tie them together securely with string, allowing a little room for expansion. Place on a heatproof plate in a large saucepan. Top up with enough boiling water just to cover the pudding, then put a lid on the pan and simmer gently for 3¾–4 hours. Check the water level occasionally and top up if necessary. You should hear the reassuring, gentle shuddering sound of the plate on the bottom of the pan for the entire duration of cooking.

Preheat the oven to 180°C/350°F/Gas 4. Wearing oven gloves, remove the pudding from the pan and dip it briefly into a bowl of cold water – for no more than 10 seconds – so the skin does not stick to the cloth. Cut the string, untie the cloth and invert the dumpling on to an ovenproof plate. Place in the oven for 10–15 minutes, just until the skin feels less sticky. Sprinkle with caster sugar and serve hot, with custard.

Bramble and Butterscotch Crumble Tart

Blackberries are always called brambles in Scotland. Whether you pick them in the wild or buy cultivated ones, try this lovely tart, which can be served warm with thick cream, clotted cream or good vanilla ice-cream. If you cannot obtain dulce de leche, an Argentinian caramel spread, use a large can of condensed milk and boil it (unopened) in a large pan of water for 2–3 hours. Keep checking the water level and top up if necessary. Leave to cool before opening.

Serves 6
1 heaped tablespoon semolina
750g/1lb 10oz brambles (blackberries)
250g/9oz dulce de leche

For the pastry:
50g/2oz golden caster sugar
75g/3oz ground almonds
150g/5oz plain flour, sifted
110g/4oz butter, diced
1 large free-range egg

For the crumble:
75g/3oz plain flour, sifted
50g/2oz medium oatmeal
75g/3oz golden granulated sugar
75g/3oz butter, diced

Make the pastry in a food processor by processing the first 4 ingredients together, then adding the egg and processing briefly to combine (or make it by hand, rubbing the butter into the dry ingredients and mixing in the egg). Once amalgamated, bring it together with your hands, wrap in clingfilm and chill well. Then roll out to fit a deep 23cm/9in loose-bottomed buttered flan tin. Prick the base and chill again for at least 3 hours, preferably overnight.

Preheat the oven to 200°C/400°F/Gas 6. Sprinkle the semolina over the pastry, then scatter over the brambles. Gently warm the dulce de leche or condensed milk and spoon it over the berries.
To make the crumble topping, mix the flour, oatmeal and sugar together and rub in the butter. Sprinkle it over the berries and press down very lightly. Bake for 15 minutes, then reduce the oven temperature to 180°C/350°F/Gas 4 and bake for a further 25 minutes, until golden brown. Leave until barely warm before carefully decanting on to a plate.

Sticky Toffee Pudding

The Udny Arms in Newburgh, Aberdeenshire, claims to be the 'spiritual home of the famous sticky toffee pudding'. It was first served in the restaurant in the late 1960s, made by cook Pauline Wood, a local resident who had apparently modified a recipe from an extremely old cookbook she had found. Indeed, I have a recipe in my 1913 *Huntly Cookery Book* (Huntly is in Aberdeenshire) for a date pudding, by Mrs McGillivray, which is made with identical ingredients but is steamed instead of baked and has no toffee sauce. Instead there is a suggestion to serve it with a 'sweet sauce'.

But then there is Sharrow Bay, the famous Lake District hotel, renowned elsewhere in Britain (but not in Aberdeenshire) as the home of sticky toffee pud. Wherein lies the answer to the conundrum? According to food writer Simon Hopkinson, the Sharrow Bay pudding dates from around 1971 and originated from a traditional Lancastrian recipe. Whatever its mysterious origins, the most important fact is that it is a truly memorable pudding, rich, dark and sticky, ideal for wintry nights in the north – of England or Scotland.

Mackies, an ice-cream producer based on the family dairy farm near Rothienorman, Aberdeenshire, makes a sticky toffee pudding ice-cream by adding treacle toffee sauce, chopped dates, sultanas and syrup to softened ice-cream. The pudding is good on its own but, for the most hedonistic experience on the pudding trolley, serve sticky toffee ice-cream or plain vanilla as well as pouring cream on top of a bowlful of hot sticky toffee pudding. You might have problems moving afterwards, however.

Here is my version of the Udny Arms recipe.

Serves 8
100g/3½oz butter, softened
200g/7oz golden caster sugar
2 large free-range eggs
450g/1lb self-raising flour, sifted
250g packet of stoned dried dates, chopped
1 teaspoon bicarbonate of soda

For the sauce:
100g/3½oz butter
200g/7oz dark muscovado sugar
300ml/10fl oz double cream

Preheat the oven to 180°C/350°F/Gas 4. Cream the butter and sugar together until fluffy, then gradually beat in the eggs. Place the dates and bicarbonate of soda in a bowl and pour over 600ml/1 pint of boiling water. Stir around well to break the dates up. Fold the flour into the butter and sugar mixture, then add the date mixture. Once well combined, tip into a 2 litre/3½ pint round ovenproof dish and bake for 45–50 minutes, until a skewer inserted into the middle comes out clean (the timing will depend on the height of your dish). Remove from the oven.

To make the sauce, bring everything to the boil in a saucepan and boil for 3–4 minutes, then pour very slowly over the pudding. You may not be able to pour over all the sauce; offer any leftovers separately in a jug. Place under a preheated grill for about 2 minutes, or until bubbling and sticky (or return to the oven on a baking sheet – it might bubble over – for 3–4 minutes). Serve hot with pouring cream or ice-cream.

Scots Trifle

There are so many variations on trifle that an entire book could be written on the subject. But I must say we have some rather fine offerings in Scotland, with our wonderful raspberries, brambles and, of course, a good supply of whisky or Drambuie to drench the sponges. This version is pretty boozy, so reduce the Drambuie by half or substitute fruit juice if children are to be involved.

Serves 8
5–6 trifle sponges, halved
raspberry jam
150g/5oz packet of ratafias
(almond macaroons)
5–6 tablespoons Drambuie
250g/9oz fresh raspberries,
plus a few extra to decorate
300ml/10fl oz double cream,
lightly whipped

For the custard:
600ml/1 pint creamy milk (or half milk,
half double cream)
25g/1oz caster sugar
4 large free-range egg yolks

First make the custard: heat the milk (or milk and cream) in a heavy saucepan until just bubbling, then remove from the heat. Beat the sugar and egg yolks together, then slowly pour them into the milk, whisking all the time. Return to a gentle heat and cook slowly, stirring or whisking, for 5–8 minutes, until slightly thickened. Do not allow it to boil or it will curdle. Leave to cool, stirring occasionally to prevent a skin forming.

Spread the trifle sponges with jam and place over the base of a pretty glass dish. Scatter over most of the ratafias, keeping some behind for decoration. Slowly sprinkle over the Drambuie until all the sponges and ratafias are just soaked; do not drown them. Top with the raspberries, then pour over the cooled custard. Cover and chill. Shortly before serving, spread with the whipped cream and decorate with ratafias and raspberries.

Cranachan

There are many different versions of this delicious – and simple – pudding. Mine includes mascarpone cheese, to give a richer texture, and I use jumbo oats instead of pinhead or coarse oatmeal. According to Scottish food historian Catherine Brown, the traditional way of eating it is to sit down at a table spread with bowls of the various ingredients and each person would mix their own cranachan in their dish, according to taste. Less whisky and more honey for the children. The traditional ingredients are simply cream, crowdie (traditional hand-skimmed cottage cheese), toasted oatmeal, fresh soft fruit such as raspberries, blaeberries and brambles, heather honey and whisky.

If you are preparing this in advance, only mix it a short time before serving, otherwise the oats will lose their crunch.

Serves 6
125g/4½oz jumbo oats (large rolled/porridge oats)
75g/3oz light muscovado sugar
250g/9oz mascarpone cheese
3–4 tablespoons malt whisky, plus extra to serve
300ml/10fl oz double cream, lightly whipped
250g/9oz raspberries
runny heather honey (optional)

Put the oats and sugar on a large sheet of foil and place under a hot grill for 3–4 minutes, stirring every 30 seconds or so. They burn quickly so watch carefully. Remove and leave to cool. Put the mascarpone in a bowl, add whisky to taste and beat until smooth. Fold this into the whipped cream with the cooled oat mixture. Once thoroughly combined, gently fold in the raspberries, taking care not to break them up. Tip into a glass bowl, cover and serve at once, or chill for no more than an hour. Offer an optional drizzle of whisky – and heather honey, if you like.

Drumlanrig Pudding

The Duchess of Buccleuch, whose Dumfriesshire home is Drumlanrig Castle, told me that until the First World War there was a huge walled garden there, with many different vegetables and fruits. Rhubarb would certainly have been a favourite and would have been cooked up regularly. Interestingly, after the great French chef, Florence (who worked for the Dukes of Buccleuch from around 1790 to 1840), almost all the cooks were women. I imagine it was one of these female chefs who transformed a regular summer pudding into a rhubarb pudding. After 24 hours in the fridge, the bread takes on a lovely pink hue from the glorious colour of the rhubarb.

Incidentally, the stunning walled garden at Drumlanrig was ploughed up and converted to the production of essential vegetables such as carrots during the Second World War, in order to feed the nation.

Serves 6

800g/1lb 12oz (trimmed weight) rhubarb, trimmed and chopped
100g/3½oz golden granulated sugar
about 200g/7oz sliced brown or wholemeal bread
(it should be fairly thickly sliced)
thick pouring cream or thick yoghurt, to serve

Put the rhubarb, sugar and 2 tablespoons of cold water in a pan, bring to the boil and simmer for 5–10 minutes, until the rhubarb is tender.

Use most of the bread to line the base and sides of a 1 litre/1¾ pint pudding basin or soufflé dish, cutting them to fit where necessary and making sure there are no gaps. Spoon in half the rhubarb, place a layer of bread on top, then top with the remaining rhubarb. Cover with a layer of bread, then put a plate or saucer on top that just fits inside the rim of the bowl. Place a weight on top of that and refrigerate for about 24 hours.

To serve, loosen the edges of the pudding with a knife and turn it out on to a plate. Serve with thick pouring cream or yoghurt sweetened with a little sugar.

Atholl Brose

Sometimes spelt Athole Brose, this is basically a drink, which I have converted into a pudding. And whereas I find the pudding delicious, served with crisp, buttery shortbread, I find it rather unpalatable as a drink – but then I am not a great whisky drinker. Shame on me, a Scot, I know!

Some versions of this ancient drink contain only honey, whisky and water. The classic recipe – credited to the fifteenth-century Duke of Atholl, who allegedly overpowered his enemies by making them drink from a well filled with this intoxicating drink – contains oatmeal, or simply the strained liquid after soaking oatmeal in water. But it was in Robert Louis Stevenson's *Kidnapped* that I found inspiration for my recipe, which has cream beaten in at the end. Stevenson writes: 'Duncan Dhu made haste to bring out the pair of pipes that was his principal possession and to set before his guests a mutton ham and a bottle of drink which they call Athole brose, and which is made of old whisky, strained honey and sweet cream, slowly beaten together in the right order and proportion.'

Serves 4
100g/3½oz medium oatmeal
2 tablespoons runny heather honey
200ml/7fl oz whisky
300ml/10fl oz double cream,
lightly whipped
shortbread, to serve

Mix the oatmeal with 200ml/7fl oz cold water and leave for 30 minutes–1 hour. Then press through a fine sieve to extract the liquid. Mix this with the honey and whisky and pour into a bottle. If using as a drink, shake well before serving.

For a pudding, gently fold 3 tablespoons of the brose into the whipped cream and transfer to a glass dish. Chill well to firm it up slightly, then serve with shortbread.

Apple Frushie

An apple frushie is an apple tart with short, crumbly pastry, the word frushie denoting the crumbly texture. I have moved this definition on a little to make a crumble instead of a tart, which is easier. This one is based on a delicious pudding I enjoyed while judging a competition in an Edinburgh girls' school. The contestant, Eve Smith, was only 11 years old yet produced one of the best crumbles – based on her grandmother's recipe – I have ever tasted.

Serves 6–8
1kg/2¼ lb cooking apples, peeled, cored
and thinly sliced
75g/3oz caster sugar

For the topping:
250g/9oz unsalted butter, diced
125g/4½oz plain flour, sifted
125g/4½oz medium oatmeal
a pinch of salt
150g/5oz light muscovado sugar

Preheat the oven to 180°C/350°F/Gas 4. Place the apples and sugar in a large ovenproof dish, stirring to coat the apples in the sugar.

To make the topping, rub the butter into the flour and oatmeal until crumbly, then stir in the salt and sugar. Tip this on to the apples and press down lightly. Bake for about 45 minutes, until the crumble is golden brown and the juices are bubbling through. Allow to cool for at least 10 minutes, then serve with vanilla ice-cream or thick cream.

Oatmeal Praline Ice-cream
with Berries

This ice-cream is divine served with berries (*au naturel*, or warmed slightly with a sprinkling of sugar until the juices run) in summer. In winter, melt some Dundee marmalade with a splash of whisky and serve this hot marmalade sauce over the ice-cream.

My recipe was inspired by F. Marian McNeill's 'Caledonian Ice', which is made by freezing sweetened whipped cream until almost hard, then stirring in some toasted coarse oatmeal. I like to make a custard-based ice-cream and fold in crunchy oatmeal praline just before churning. Although home-made is best, if you are feeling lazy you could simply mix the praline into a 1–litre tub of softened good-quality bought vanilla ice-cream.

Serves 6–8
500ml/18fl oz full-fat milk
300ml/10fl oz double cream
4 large free-range egg yolks
125g/4½oz caster sugar
seasonal berries, such as brambles, blaeberries and raspberries, to serve

For the praline:
150g/5oz pinhead oatmeal
140g tub of liquid glucose syrup
125g/4½oz caster sugar

Put the milk and cream in a heavy-based saucepan and bring slowly to the boil. Meanwhile, beat together the egg yolks and sugar until smooth. Just before they reach boiling point, pour the milk and cream over the egg and sugar mixture, stirring all the time. Then tip it back into the pan and return to a low heat. Stirring constantly, cook gently for about 10 minutes or until it has the consistency of double cream. It will thicken on cooling, so don't panic and think it is too thin. Leave to cool, stirring frequently to prevent a skin forming.

For the praline, toast the oatmeal either under the grill for a couple of minutes or in an oven preheated to 180°C/350°F/Gas 4 for 8–10 minutes, just until it smells nutty and toasty. If you use the grill, watch the oatmeal to make sure it does not burn. Tip it on to an oiled baking sheet. Place the glucose and sugar in a heavy-based saucepan and stir over a low heat until the sugar dissolves. Dip a pastry brush in cold water and brush quickly down the inside of the pan to loosen any sugar that is stuck to the sides. Then, without stirring at all, allow the mixture to bubble away for 8–10 minutes or until it is golden brown colour. During this time, swirl the pan around a couple of times. Then pour the mixture over the oatmeal, trying to cover it – but don't worry if the oatmeal is not all covered. Leave to cool, then break up and place in a food processor. Using the pulse button, process to coarse crumbs. Don't process too long or it will be powdery.

Once the custard is cold, stir in the praline, then pour into an ice-cream machine and churn. Or pour into a large, shallow freezer container, seal and place in the freezer. Remove after 2 hours, whisk madly (this helps prevent ice crystals forming) and return to the freezer. Repeat the whisking a couple of times, then freeze until firm.

To serve, transfer from freezer to fridge for about 20 minutes or until slightly softened. Serve with berries.

Whisky and Honey Ice-Cream

The character of this ice-cream alters completely depending on which whisky you use. I recommend either a Speyside or a Lowland one, not an Islay one: the peaty taste would dominate. The ice-cream packs a powerful punch. Serve it on its own, with poached apricots or fresh strawberries, or place a scoop on top of a hot pudding such as Sticky Toffee Pudding (see page 128) or Cloutie Dumpling (see page 124). Not traditional, I grant you, but exceedingly welcome nonetheless.

Serves 6
500ml/18fl oz full-fat milk
300ml/10fl oz double cream
2 tablespoons heather honey
4 large free-range egg yolks
100g/3½oz golden caster sugar
2 tablespoons malt whisky

Place the milk, cream and honey in a heavy-based saucepan and bring slowly to the boil. Beat the egg yolks and sugar together until smooth, then stir a little of the milk mixture into the yolks. Pour this into the pan and cook over a low heat, stirring constantly, for about 10 minutes, until slightly thickened. Don't let it boil or it will curdle. Pour the mixture into a jug and leave to cool completely, stirring occasionally to prevent a skin forming.

Once the custard is cold, stir in the whisky, then pour into an ice-cream machine and churn. Or pour into a large, shallow freezer container, cover and freeze – preferably on fast-freeze – for 6 hours, removing every 2 hours to whisk madly (this helps prevent ice crystals forming). Transfer the ice-cream to the fridge to soften up a little before serving.

Carragheen Pudding

Carragheen or Irish moss (*Chondrus crispus*) is found all round the British coastline and is used particularly in Scottish and Irish seaside towns and villages. Its gelatinous quality is useful for setting jellies and blancmange-style puddings, and it is often added to commercial ice-creams and jellies.

In the Hebrides many seaweeds are used as fertilisers, to enhance the flavour of new potatoes. A nourishing drink made by adding dried powdered carragheen to hot milk or water was popular in the Hebrides, especially as it had sedative qualities.

In the coastal Highlands, a restorative jelly made with carragheen used to be given to invalids. A milk pudding similar to the one below was also prescribed for those suffering from chest complaints, bronchitis or asthma because of its high mineral content, particularly iodine.

Flavourings such as rosewater, citrus zest or juice (Seville oranges being particularly good) and, of course, sugar can be added according to taste. I personally like it plain, perhaps served with some stewed rhubarb, which is the way Auchmithie cook Margaret Horn has eaten it all her life.

If using dried carragheen, you will need a minimum of 10g/½oz and it should be soaked in water for 15 minutes first.

Serves 6

50g/2oz freshly picked carragheen, well washed

1 litre/1¾ pints full-fat milk

sugar and other flavourings (optional)

Bring the carragheen and milk slowly to the boil, then simmer for 30–40 minutes or until the seaweed has become rather gelatinous. Add any flavourings now – sugar to taste, a dash of rosewater or some lemon or orange juice. Strain into a bowl and leave somewhere cold to set.

Eat on its own or with stewed rhubarb or apples.

9
baking

Another name for this chapter could be Teabreads, which, in many parts of Scotland, encompasses all manner of cakes, buns, biscuits, tarts, scones and fruit loaves. Teabreads are what you have with tea – after a simple hot dish such as eggs, smoked ('yellow') fish or oatmeal herring. In Aberdeenshire, a 'fly cup' (of tea) is invariably accompanied by a 'fine piece', which means something extremely tasty, usually sweet, often home-baked.

Home-baking is something we Scots have always excelled at, although, strangely, often without the use of an oven. F. Marian McNeill in her 1929 book, *The Scots Kitchen*, wrote, 'In Scotland, amongst the rural population generally, the girdle takes the place of the oven, the bannock of the loaf.'

But although the oven came into the Scots kitchen much later than the girdle, our skills at cakes, tarts and oven scones have come on apace with our innate girdle skills. Girdle is the Scots word for griddle. If you do not have a cast-iron girdle (griddle) you can use a heavy-based frying pan instead, although the heat distribution is not as even and it is not as practical to flip things over. I also find there is less chance of girdle scones or bannocks browning too much on a girdle, as it cooks them more quickly.

Sadly, nowadays, many people use neither girdle nor oven to bake. How deprived their tastebuds must be, for baking is one of life's greatest pleasures. It is also surely the most selfless of culinary arts, since it is all about sharing. Cakes, shortbread and scones are not only for the cook (although one of the great perks is scraping the bowl), they are made to be enjoyed by others.

Even if you have not done much baking before, I urge you to try some of the easy recipes in this chapter. The only proviso is that you must use good-quality ingredients: best butter for the shortbread, fine, plump raisins for the Border tart and rich, treacly dark muscovado sugar for the Ecclefechan tart. Then, once you have made some of the most intriguing-sounding recipes in the book – puggy buns, fatty cuties, broonie – all you have to do is sit back and wait for them to cool as the fabulously alluring smells of home-baking fill your house.

Scotch Pancakes

This is fast food as it was meant to be. From mixing the ingredients for these delicious little pancakes (called drop scones outside Scotland) to eating them warm takes as little as 10 minutes.

This is based on my mother's recipe, as it was part of her weekly repertoire, along with guggy cake (a boiled fruit cake), treacle scones and sultana cake. Sometimes the pancakes would be spread with raspberry jam, sometimes apple or blackcurrant jelly – all home-made. They are best eaten immediately but you could make a batch and freeze it for some later date. To reheat, thaw slightly, then wrap in foil and place in a moderate oven.

If you have never used a girdle before, it is easy: test whether it is hot enough by dropping a teaspoonful of the batter on to the surface. It should set almost at once and begin to bubble after 1 minute. It is the large bubbles that tell you the pancakes are ready to be flipped over. Those – and a growing impatience to devour the entire batch at once sitting – are the clue that it's time to put the kettle on, for tea is about to be served.

Makes 12–16
110g/4oz plain flour, sifted
½ teaspoon cream of tartar
¼ teaspoon bicarbonate of soda
a pinch of salt
1 teaspoon golden caster sugar
1 medium free-range egg, beaten
150ml/5fl oz milk
a little butter for the girdle

Sift the first 4 ingredients into a bowl. Stir in the sugar, then make a well in the middle. Add the egg and whisk together with a balloon whisk, then gradually add the milk, whisking all the time.

Continue whisking until you have a smooth batter. Heat the girdle (or a large heavy frying pan) over a medium heat. Using a wad of kitchen paper, smear a thin film of butter all over it. Once it is hot – mine takes about 3 minutes to heat up – drop spoonfuls of batter on to the girdle, 4 at a time. If you want dainty little ones, use a dessertspoon; for slightly larger ones, use a tablespoon. After about 1½–2 minutes you will notice large bubbles forming on top. Using a spatula, flip each one over and continue cooking for a further 1–1½ minutes until just done. They should take about 3 minutes altogether.

Remove and keep warm in a folded tea towel while you cook the rest. Serve with butter – and jam if you like.

Treacle Scones

I have always loved treacle puddings and bakes. Black treacle is popular in Scotland, whether in steamed puddings, gingerbread or scones.

As a child I had a different type of treacle scone at Hallowe'en. Then we would attempt to bite thick, floury, triangular scones that had been daubed in sticky black treacle. The snag was that they were hung by a string from the washing line in the kitchen (above a newspaper-lined floor, needless to say!) and our hands were tied behind our backs. Thankfully the next game was always dooking for apples, which involved immersion in tubs of freezing cold water to try and bite apples that always managed to bob away from you just as you were about to pounce. How come I recall these games as fun?

Makes 6–8
50g/2oz unsalted butter
1 heaped tablespoon black treacle
225g/8oz self-raising flour
a pinch of salt
½ teaspoon ground ginger
½ teaspoon mixed spice
about 50–70ml/2–2½fl oz milk

Preheat the oven to 220°C/425°F/Gas 7. Put the butter and treacle in a small pan over a low heat until just melted, then remove from the heat and leave to cool for about 5 minutes. Sift the flour, salt and spices into a mixing bowl. Make a well in the centre, then pour in the treacle and butter mixture with just enough milk to combine to a fairly soft dough. Add 3 tablespoons of milk at first, then add more if necessary.

With lightly floured hands, bring the dough together, using a very light touch with minimal handling, otherwise the scones will be tough. Pat out to a thickness of about 2cm/¾in (do not use a rolling pin). If there are any cracks, knead gently together until smooth. Using fluted or round scone cutters, cut out 6–8 scones. Place these on a buttered baking sheet and bake for about 10 minutes, until well risen. Transfer to a wire rack to cool a little, before eating warm with butter.

Aggie's Scones

My friend Aggie MacKenzie from Rothiemurchus has always raved about her granny's scone recipe, which she bakes frequently. Ina Campbell, Aggie's grandmother, handed on the recipe to Aggie's mum, who used to win prizes at all the local shows for her scones. The name Ina was short for Angusina and this adding on of Ina to any male's name in the family was traditional in the Sutherland area, where Ina Campbell came from. Aggie has an aunt called Hughina and a more distant relative called Hectorina Donaldina. Some traditions are better relegated to history . . . unlike the scone recipe, which is absolutely the best!

Makes 15–16

450g/1lb plain flour
1 heaped teaspoon bicarbonate of soda
1 rounded teaspoon cream of tartar
1 heaped teaspoon salt
40g/1½oz butter
1 tablespoon golden syrup
1 large free-range egg
300ml/10fl oz full-fat milk

Preheat the oven to its highest setting – 240°C/475°F/Gas 9. Sift the flour into a bowl with the soda, tartar and salt. Melt the butter and syrup together and cool slightly, then tip into the bowl. Beat the egg into the milk and add to the flour mixture. Stir together until combined to a soft dough, then, using well-floured hands, turn the dough on to a floured board and flattened gently to about 2.5cm/1in thick. The dough is very soft, so keep lightly flouring both hands and board. Cut out with a floured scone cutter and place on a very lightly greased hot baking sheet (I place it in the oven as it is heating up). Bake for 7–8 minutes, then transfer to a wire rack. Eat barely warm, with butter and jam.

Fatty Cutties

The fatty cuttie is a northern relative of those other famous girdle cakes, the Singin' Hinnie of Northumberland and the Welsh cake. My recipe was given to me by Mrs Scott, who used to live on the northerly Orkney island of Westray. It is similar to a recipe from Mrs Mathers of Stenness, in the west mainland of Orkney, but the mainland one uses double the amount of butter. Perhaps this is an indication of the relative affluence on the mainland.

According to Mrs Scott, the Orcadian fatty cuttie originated many years ago when people were very poor indeed. Daily bread took the form of a girdle bannock, usually made from beremeal. As people became slightly better off they began to use wheat flour instead of barley and also began to add fat (butter) to their girdle breads and cakes. Eventually the cakes came to be known as fatty cutties because they were enriched with fat and because they were cut into wedges before baking. A similar dish is the Shetland fatty brunnies, which are thick cakes of oatmeal and/or wheat flour baked on the girdle and enriched with a lump of lard to keep them soft.

Makes 8
175g/6oz plain flour
¼ teaspoon bicarbonate of soda
75g/3oz caster sugar
75g/3oz currants
75g/3oz butter, melted
about 1 tablespoon milk
a little butter for the girdle

Sift the flour and bicarbonate of soda into a mixing bowl. Stir in the sugar and currants, then pour in the melted butter and just enough milk to combine to a stiff dough. You may need to add another ½–1 tablespoon of milk. Knead very lightly and divide into 2 balls.

On a lightly floured surface, roll each ball into a circle, about 5mm/¼in thick, then cut into 4 wedges. Heat your girdle to medium-hot, grease very lightly, using a wad of kitchen paper, then cook the fatty cutties for 3–4 minutes on each side, until golden brown. Serve warm without butter or cold with a thin smear of butter.

Shortbread

When I was *assistante* in a *lycée* in the Pyrenees, I often made shortbread for the pupils and staff. They absolutely loved it but always said how rich it was. This had never occurred to me, for it was such a part of my life that I just took it for what it was – simple and delicious, yet almost mundane. But considering it was originally a special-occasion biscuit (unlike the plainer bannocks and oatcakes), which has gradually become mainstream, it is not really surprising that first-timers consider it rich.

In her book on the Scots household in the eighteenth century, Marion Lochhead writes about tea parties of the day where the hostess 'must have a plate of bun and one of shortbread – either in a cake, broken into bits, or in little, round nickety Tantallon cakes, or in the favourite "petticoat tails". (I have no idea what nickety means either!) Many years on, shortbread still appears at all the best tea parties and also on special occasions such as Hogmanay (with black bun) but is also as regular a feature in Scottish kitchens as porridge or mince.

The following recipe is from my Granny Anderson's recipe book and my Auntie Muriel has dated it 14 January 1947. No one can recall this being a special occasion but the two brothers and two sisters were all back from their war duties and were living at home together once again. Feeding six adults every night must have been hard work but my grandmother was a strong character, having brought up four children pretty much on her own while her husband was away at sea. Shortbread would have been one of many items filling the biscuits tins, baked either by granny or her daughters, for visitors or family tea.

My granny's recipe is a rather frugal one – many recipes give a higher ratio of butter to flour. For a richer shortbread, see Petticoat Tails on page 148 or Moira MacAulay's Shortbread on page 149. All are exceptionally easy to make but only the best ingredients will give a good buttery, crumbly finish. Instead of semolina you could use rice flour (ground rice) for a similarly crunchy texture. Or use fine semolina (farola) or cornflour for a more melt-in-

the-mouth feel. Simplest of all, of course, is to use only flour.

Remember that shortbread should never be kneaded for longer than it takes to bring the dough together quickly in your hands. Overworking it will toughen the shortbread. Indeed I never roll it with a rolling pin, I just press it out lightly to the required shape before baking. The lightest hand will give the lightest shortbread.

Makes about 16 pieces
110g/4oz slightly salted butter, softened
50g/2oz caster sugar
175g/6oz plain flour, sifted
50g/2oz semolina
caster sugar, for dredging

Preheat the oven to 170°C/325°F/Gas 3. Cream the butter and sugar together, then gradually add the flour and semolina. Bring together with your hands and knead briefly to combine to a ball. Using your fingers, lightly press it out to a rectangle, about 5mm/¼in thick, then cut it into fingers (it can also be pressed into two 20cm/8in sandwich tins or a shortbread mould). Place on a greased baking tray and prick lightly all over with a fork, then bake for about 20 minutes or until pale golden brown. Dredge with caster sugar and transfer to a wire rack to cool.

Variations
Highlanders: shape the dough into a long roll, roll this in milk then demerara sugar and cut into slices before baking.

Tantallon cakes: use rice flour instead of semolina, add the grated zest of 1 small lemon and cut into round biscuits.

Yetholm bannock: add 1 heaped tablespoon of chopped crystallised ginger and an egg yolk to the basic dough, which should be baked in an oblong.

Pitcaithly bannock: add 1 tablespoon each of chopped almonds and candied peel to the dough and bake in a large round.

Oaties

These deliciously crunchy oat biscuits are based on ones made by the Shortbread House of Edinburgh, which makes superb shortbread and other biscuits, all by hand. Obviously the staff were not keen to divulge its recipe but mine is cobbled together from their ingredients list – and lots of sneaky tastings! My biscuits are slightly less 'short' in texture. Both have their merits; both are good with tea or coffee.

Makes 18–20
110g/4oz butter
50g/2oz golden caster sugar
2 level tablespoons golden syrup
125g/4½oz rolled oats
75g/3oz plain flour, sifted
½ teaspoon bicarbonate of soda
100g/3½oz desiccated coconut

Preheat the oven to 180°C/350°F/Gas 4.
Melt the butter, sugar and syrup together in a large pan, then stir in the oats, flour, bicarbonate of soda and coconut. Drop spoonfuls of the mixture on to 2 greased baking sheets and bake for 12–15 minutes, until golden. Leave on the baking sheets for 2 minutes, then transfer to a wire rack to cool and firm up.

Petticoat Tails

This is just one of several recipes for petticoat tails. You could use all flour (no semolina) or substitute regular semolina for the farola if this is hard to find. Some old recipes suggest adding caraway seeds – a throwback to the days when caraway comfits (caraway seeds thickly coated in boiled sugar) were widely used as decoration.

Some believe that the name of these dainty shortbread biscuits is a corruption of the French *petites galettes*, meaning little cakes. Given the culinary interchange between France and Scotland, this is a possibility. But what is also possible is that the biscuits were named for their shape: they are identical to the individual gores of the full, bell-hooped petticoats worn by ladies at Court – probably in the sixteenth century at the time of Mary, Queen of Scots, who was said to be fond of them.

The classic shape of petticoat tails is a round with a small inner circle removed and wedges cut all the way around it. It is, of course, easier just to mark it into sixths or eighths, but if you wish to follow the traditional method, proceed according to the instructions in F. Marian McNeill's *The Scots Kitchen*:

'Cut out the cake by running a paste-cutter round a dinner plate or any large round dish inverted on the paste. Cut a cake from the centre of this one with a small saucer or large tumbler. Keep this inner circle whole and cut the outer one into eight petticoat-tails. Bake all these on paper laid on tins, serve the round cake in the middle of the plate, and the petticoat tails as radii round it.'

Makes 12–18
175g/6oz slightly salted butter
50g/2oz caster sugar
175g/6oz plain flour
50g/2oz farola (fine semolina)
caster sugar, for dredging

Preheat the oven to 150°C/300°F/Gas 2. Cream the butter and sugar together, then sift in the flour and farola. Mix together and knead very briefly until combined. Divide in 2 (or 3) and lightly press the pieces into two 20cm/8in (or three 15cm/6in) greased sandwich tins. Prick all over with a fork. Bake for 30–40 minutes or until pale golden brown. Remove from the oven and cut each round into 6 or 8 wedges. Dredge with caster sugar and leave to cool before decanting on to a wire rack.

Moira MacAulay's Shortbread

Moira MacAulay, mother of my university friend, comedian Fred MacAulay, bakes her shortbread regularly, to great acclaim. Fred's eldest son, Jack, declares Granny Moira's shortbread to be the best in Scotland — I am inclined to agree.

Moira insists there is no secret. In fact she developed her own recipe from one on the back of a cornflour packet many years ago. But she does insist that a really good, well-used baking tin is essential. Hers — an ancient one given to her by an aunt — is already the subject of fierce dispute between her daughters-in-law. Never mind the family jewels, who will inherit the shortbread tin?

Makes 20–24 pieces
225g/8oz butter
(I use slightly salted), softened
110g/4oz caster sugar
(I use golden caster)
225g/8oz plain flour, sifted
150g/5oz cornflour, sifted
caster sugar, for dredging

Preheat the oven to 150°C/300°F/Gas 2. Place the butter and sugar in a mixer or food processor and cream until pale. Add the flour and cornflour and blend briefly, just until thoroughly combined. Tip into a buttered 23 x 33cm/9 x 13in swiss roll tin and, using floured hands, press down so it is level. Prick it all over with a fork (do this carefully, so that you do not disturb the level surface), then bake for 50–60 minutes (Moira bakes hers for 1 hour; my oven requires only 50 minutes). It should be a uniform pale golden colour all over; do not allow it to become golden brown.

Remove from the oven and dredge all over with caster sugar, then cut into squares. Leave for 5 minutes or so, then carefully decant on to a wire rack to cool.

Parlies

Parlies are a type of gingerbread baked as biscuits. Although soft when you remove them from the oven, they firm up as they cool to become crisp but slightly chewy in the centre. It is important not to overwork the dough or they will be tough.

The name is short for parliament cakes, and it is said to derive from their popularity with members of the Scots parliament. In late-eighteenth-century Edinburgh, a lady called Mrs Flockhart ran a shop and tavern in Potterrow, at the back of what is now the Royal Scottish Museum in Chambers Street. Although the shop was a general one, the back room was the scene of her most profitable business. Her eminent customers – including Mr Scott (father of Sir Walter) and several Lords – would pass through the shop to the back room to partake of a dram or two and some gingerbread or biscuits. Her thin, crisp, square cakes were parliaments or parlies, the round ones snaps and the thick soft cakes were called white or brown quality cakes. I wonder if parlies are set to make a comeback now that Scotland has its own parliament again . . .

Fife's equivalent to parlies is paving stones (known as paving stanes). These are made from a gingerbread-type mixure that is shaped into old-fashioned oblong cobble shapes. After baking, a boiled sugar syrup is poured over them to form a crunchy coating.

Makes 4 extra-large or 16 small squares
110g/4oz unsalted butter
2 heaped tablespoons black treacle
225g/8oz plain flour
1 rounded teaspoon ground ginger
a pinch of salt
50g/2oz dark muscovado sugar

Preheat the oven to 170°C/325°F/Gas 3. Melt the butter and treacle together gently. Sift the flour, ginger and salt into a bowl and stir in the sugar. Pour in the melted mixture and stir briefly to combine.

Tip into a shallow 23cm/9in square buttered cake tin and, using floured hands, flatten down. Prick all over with a fork and bake for 20 minutes. Remove from the oven and cut into squares, then, while still warm, decant carefully on to a wire rack to cool. They will firm up as they cool.

Puggy Buns

Probably the oldest bakery in the UK, Adamson's of Pittenweem, was established in 1635 by a Dutchman called Hedderwick (this is doubtless an anglicised spelling). The East Neuk of Fife, which incorporates Pittenweem and other charming villages such as St Monans, Anstruther and Crail, used to trade regularly with Holland: the Dutch wanted Fife's potatoes, the Scots wanted Holland's wonderful tiles for their houses. The tiny bakery stands adjacent to the old Pittenweem castle (built some 10 years before the bakery), where Charles I dined on a visit to Scotland in 1635. Hedderwick was asked to bake something special to mark the occasion and the Hedderwick bun was born. When I asked the bakery owner, Kenny Adamson, for the recipe he looked at me as if I was mad. This was a secret that would possibly go with him to the grave. Then I asked if it was something like a Selkirk bannock, for it looks and tastes similar. His reply: 'You could say the Selkirk bannock is like the Hedderwick bun.'

But he did give me a recipe for another extremely old, traditional bun, the puggy bun. These look vaguely similar to Eccles cakes or Chorley cakes, although they don't contain dried fruit. They have been made in Adamson's bakery for many years – certainly since Kenny's grandmother, Agnes, bought the bakery in 1887. The old Scotch oven with the classic beehive roof is still in perfect working order, although it now runs on oil, not coal. The puggy buns, which are known locally as hypocrites – black inside, white outside – are filled with a gingerbread-type mixture called a gundy dough. Gundy is the old Scots word for a spiced confection or sweetmeat. The gundy dough can be made in advance and will keep for several weeks in an airtight container in the fridge. The outer dough used to be a barm dough, then later yeast dough, but now shortcrust pastry is used.

These Fife specialities can be enjoyed plain or spread with butter. Kenny likes to warm his under the grill before buttering.

Makes 6
275g/10oz plain flour, sifted
a pinch of salt
110g/4oz butter

For the gundy:
175g/6oz strong white flour
3 heaped tablespoons golden syrup, warmed
50g/2oz golden caster sugar
1 heaped teaspoon bicarbonate of soda
1 heaped teaspoon mixed spice
50ml/2fl oz milk

Make the gundy first: sift the flour into a bowl, add all the other ingredients and stir with a wooden spoon to combine. Wrap in clingfilm, then chill.

For the pastry, put all the ingredients in a food processor and process briefly until the mixture resembles breadcrumbs. Add enough cold water to make a firm dough – about 75ml/3fl oz. Wrap in clingfilm and chill for an hour or so. Preheat the oven to 190°C/375°F/Gas 5.

Roll out the pastry thinly and cut out six circles, about 15cm/6in in diameter. Divide the gundy into 6 and place a portion in the centre of each circle. Fold in the edges and pinch them together to seal, then turn over. Roll out each one with a rolling pin to form a rough circle about 10cm/4in in diameter. Place on a greased baking tray and slit the top of each bun 3 times. Bake for 20–25 minutes, until pale golden brown. Transfer to a wire rack to cool.

Orkney Broonie

Not to be confused with Shetland's fatty brunnies, which are thick girdle scones or bannocks made of wholemeal flour or oatmeal, the Orkney broonie is a light, moist gingerbread, not dissimilar to Yorkshire or Lancashire parkin. Both brunnie and broonie come from an old Norse word, *bruni*, which, according to F. Marian McNeill, means a thick bannock.

The broonie keeps well, wrapped in foil, and is good either plain or buttered, with a cup of tea. Or warm up thick slices and serve with butterscotch sauce and a great dollop of clotted cream for a truly memorable pudding.

Makes 1 Loaf
175g/6oz medium oatmeal
175g/6oz self-raising flour, sifted
a pinch of salt
85g/3¼ oz unsalted butter, diced
1 heaped teaspoon ground ginger
85g/3¼ oz light muscovado sugar
2 rounded tablespoons black treacle
1 medium free-range egg, beaten
150ml/5fl oz buttermilk (or fresh milk soured with ½ teaspoon lemon juice)

Preheat the oven to 170°C/325°F/Gas 3. Combine the oatmeal, flour and salt in a bowl. Rub in the butter, then stir in the ginger and sugar. Place the treacle in a small pan and heat very gently, then stir in the egg. Pour this mixture into the dry ingredients with the buttermilk or milk. Stir until thoroughly combined, then pour into a buttered, base-lined 900g/2lb loaf tin. Bake for 60–70 minutes, until a skewer inserted into the middle comes out clean. Set the tin on a wire rack and leave until cold before turning out.

Sultana Cake

It all came back to me as I licked the bowl. There I was, aged four, maybe five, kneeling on a kitchen stool and scraping my mother's mixing bowl just after she had put her sultana cake into the oven. Like tea loaf, scones and pancakes (the Scotch variety), sultana cake was available almost daily and so this was a frequent occurrence. And yet there was still something magical about climbing on to the stool and licking the bowl. Cynics among you might call it greed. I call it sharing baking duties – and, of course, quality time, had it existed in those days – with my mother. Afterwards we had to wait for the cake to be ready and, most agonising of all, wait for it to cool while the comforting smell of warm cake filled the house.

My mother cannot eat sultanas any more and she says this cake is one of the simple pleasures she misses. As I revisited my childhood, baking my mother's sultana cake after far too many years, I began to understand how she feels.

Makes a 18cm/7in cake
175g/6oz butter, softened
175g/6oz golden caster sugar
3 medium free-range eggs
225g/8oz plain flour, sifted
225g/8oz sultanas
1 level dessertspoon golden granulated sugar

Preheat the oven to 170°C/325°F/Gas 3. Cream the butter and sugar together until pale. Beat in the eggs one at a time, with a third of the flour after each addition. Stir in the sultanas and combine well to make a fairly stiff dough. Turn into a buttered, base-lined, deep 18cm/7in cake tin and bake for about 1 hour or until a cocktail stick or skewer inserted in the centre comes out clean. Switch off the oven and sprinkle the top of the cake with the granulated sugar. Return to the oven for 3–4 minutes, then transfer to a wire rack to cool. Turn out of the tin when cold.

Dundee Cake

Dundee is famous for many things. Besides its marmalade and its pies, there is the cake. Dundee cake is known throughout the world but, strangely enough, it is seldom eaten in Dundee. It is one of those things – rather like haggis – which, although meant to represent the Scottish people's daily fare, is eaten only on high days and holidays. The rich ingredients would have made it an expensive cake for the average Dundee citizen.

Having said that, it is a cake to be proud of and its origins – according to David Goodfellow of Goodfellow & Steven (one of Scotland's best bakeries, established in Dundee in 1897) – are closely linked to the marmalade industry. The surplus of orange peel from Keiller's marmalade was used in Dundee cakes. A sign, therefore, of an authentic Dundee cake is the use of orange peel rather than mixed peel. Unless you are a purist, however, good-quality mixed peel will still make a very fine cake.

A well-made Dundee cake is a good alternative to a richer, darker Christmas cake and is also ideal for afternoon tea. It keeps well, tightly wrapped in a tin.

Makes a 18cm/7in cake
175g/6oz unsalted butter, softened
175g/6oz golden caster sugar
grated zest of 1 small orange
4 medium free-range eggs
175g/6oz plain flour
1 level teaspoon baking powder
½ teaspoon mixed spice (optional)
50g/2oz ground almonds
110g/4oz sultanas
110g/4oz raisins
110g/4oz currants
50g/2oz candied orange peel, chopped
about 1 tablespoon brandy or whisky
16–20 whole blanched almonds

Preheat the oven to 150°C/300°F/Gas 2. Cream together the butter and sugar until pale, add the orange zest, then beat in the eggs one at a time, adding a little flour if the mixture looks like curdling. Sift in the flour, baking powder and mixed spice, if using, then add the ground almonds. Fold in gently but thoroughly. Stir in the dried fruit and candied peel, with enough brandy or whisky to make a slightly soft consistency.

Spoon into a greased and lined deep 18cm/7in cake tin and smooth the top. Bake for 2½–3 hours, until a toothpick or skewer inserted in the centre comes out clean. Halfway through baking, remove from the oven, arrange the almonds on top and then return to the oven. Place a piece of foil loosely over the top if it becomes too brown during the last half hour or so. Cool completely in the tin before turning out.

Selkirk Bannock

Reputedly a favourite teatime treat of Queen Victoria, this rich, fruited sweet bread is a speciality of the Borders. It originated in the town of Selkirk as a means of using up spare bread dough. Good Selkirk bannocks are now made by bakers in other Border towns, such as Galashiels, Hawick and Kelso. Although some add the butter at the beginning when making up the dough, I prefer to follow the basic guidelines in F. Marian McNeill's *The Scots Kitchen*:

'Get 2 pounds of dough from the baker. Into this rub 4 ounces butter and 4 ounces of lard until melted but not oiled. Then work in ½ pound of sugar, ¾ pound sultanas and ¼ pound chopped orange peel. Put the dough into a buttered tin, let it stand for 30 minutes to rise then bake in a good steady oven.'

For those of us unable to buy 2 pounds of dough from the baker, here is my version for – I must say – a truly magnificent bannock that is easy to make and all too easy to consume. Since I am not keen on peel, I prefer to use sultanas alone. Besides, according to Theodora Fitzgibbon's *A Taste of Scotland*, it was originally made only with the finest Turkish sultanas. Orange or mixed peel seems to be a rather more recent addition – recent being a relative term, since *The Scots Kitchen* was published in 1929.

Makes 1 large bannock
900g/2lb strong white flour
a pinch of salt
2 x 7g sachets of easy-blend dried yeast
50g/2oz caster sugar
about 500ml/18fl oz warm semi-skimmed milk (or half milk, half water)
150g/5oz butter, softened
400g/14oz sultanas
1 medium free-range egg, beaten, to glaze

Sift the flour and salt into a bowl, then stir in the yeast and sugar. Add enough warm milk to combine to a soft but not sticky dough. Turn on to a floured board and knead well for 10 minutes or so, until smooth. Place in a bowl, cover and leave somewhere warm for 1–1½ hours, until well risen.

Cut the softened butter in 4. Flatten the dough, place a piece of butter in the centre and fold the dough over, then knead until thoroughly amalgamated. Repeat with the remaining butter. Work in the sultanas, a handful at a time. Shape into a bannock: a round, flattened dome about 28cm/11in diameter. Place on a buttered baking sheet, glaze with some of the beaten egg and leave, uncovered, for about an hour, until well risen. Preheat the oven to 220°C/425°F/Gas 7.

Glaze the bannock with the remaining egg and bake for 15 minutes. Then reduce the oven temperature to 190°C/375°F/Gas 5 and cook for a further 25–30 minutes, covering loosely with foil for the last 15–20 minutes to prevent the top burning. It is ready when it is golden brown all over and the base sounds hollow when tapped underneath. Leave to cool on a wire rack. Serve sliced and spread with butter.

Border Tart

This is based on one of my mother's teatime specials. These days, Border tart is a shortcrust pastry case filled with a rich, spiced raisin filling, to which I add grated lemon zest. Originally it was made with an enriched bread dough and filled with almonds, raisins, peel and marzipan, all bound together in an egg custard. The dough for the base would have been a portion taken from the weekly breadmaking.

Similar tarts can be found all over the Borders, most noticeably Eyemouth tart, which is also made with raisins and brown sugar but includes coconut, walnuts and glacé cherries, too. Ecclefechan Tart (see page 160) is another variation on the theme. Ecclefechan is just over the south-west border of the Borders, and so is a local variation gone somewhat astray.

Serves 8
100g/3½oz unsalted butter, softened
100g/3½oz dark muscovado sugar
2 large free-range eggs, beaten
400g/14oz raisins
grated zest of 1 large lemon
1 teaspoon mixed spice

For the pastry:
150g/5oz plain flour, sifted
50g/2oz ground almonds
125g/4½oz unsalted butter, diced
20g/¾oz caster sugar
a pinch of salt
1 large free-range egg, beaten

To make the pastry, place the flour, almonds, butter, sugar and salt in a food processor and process until the mixture resembles breadcrumbs. Add the egg and process briefly. Bring the mixture together with your hands, wrap in clingfilm and chill for 1 hour. Roll out the pastry and use to line a 23cm/9in tart tin. Prick the base all over with a fork and chill for at least 2 hours, preferably overnight.

Preheat the oven to 200°C/400°F/Gas 6. Line the pastry case with foil, fill with baking beans and bake for 10 minutes, then remove the foil and beans and bake for 5 minutes longer. Remove from the oven and reduce the temperature to 190°C/375°F/Gas 5.

For the filling, beat together the butter and sugar, then stir in the eggs, raisins, lemon zest and spice. Tip this into the part-baked pastry case, return to the oven and bake for 30 minutes, until set. You might need to cover the tart loosely with foil for the last 10 minutes or so to prevent the raisins burning. Leave the tart to cool, then serve in slices with tea or coffee.

Holyrood Tart

Since 1966, John Young has run the Breadalbane Bakery in Aberfeldy, where dozens of Holyrood tarts are baked and sold every week. He brought the recipe with him from Leven, in Fife, where he served his apprenticeship, but the Aberfeldy bakery is now the only one in Scotland baking these tarts. Similar to Border and Eyemouth tarts, they differ by having a lattice piped across the top to keep the fruit moist. Mr Young makes the lattice from a soft Viennese mixture but I have adapted his basic recipe to one with a stiffer lattice dough that can be cut instead of piped. I appreciate piping is not everyone's cup of tea.

Serves 6–8

75g/3oz sultanas

50g/2oz currants

25g/1oz glacé cherries, roughly chopped

50g/2oz walnuts, roughly chopped

1 heaped tablespoon pineapple jam

1 level tablespoon golden syrup

50ml/2fl oz water

2 tablespoons icing sugar, sifted

For the pastry:

225g/8oz plain flour, sifted

110g/4oz butter, diced

25g/1oz granulated sugar

For the lattice:

110g/4oz butter, softened

225g/8oz icing sugar, sifted

75g/3oz plain flour, sifted

First prepare the filling. Place the dried fruit, cherries, walnuts, jam, golden syrup and water in a saucepan and heat slowly until both jam and syrup have melted. Leave to cool (by which time the fruit will have swollen).

Make the pastry in a food processor by processing the flour, butter and sugar together, then adding about 50ml/2fl oz cold water to bind. (Alternatively make it by hand: rub the butter into the flour, stir in the sugar, then the water.) Wrap in clingfilm and chill for an hour or so, then roll it out and use to line a 23cm/9in tart tin, prick all over with a fork and chill again.

To make the lattice, cream the butter and icing sugar together, then gradually mix in the flour. Clingfilm and chill briefly.

Preheat the oven to 200°C/400°F/Gas 6. Spread the cooled filling over the pastry base. Roll out the lattice dough to form a large rectangle. Cut it into 6 long strips and use these to make a rough lattice. Don't worry if it is not beautiful – it spreads out a little as it bakes anyway. Bake for about 25 minutes, until golden. Meanwhile, make a simple glacé icing by mixing the icing sugar with 2 teaspoons of cold water. When the tart emerges from the oven, drizzle this all over the top. Eat at room temperature.

Ecclefechan Tart

Similar to Border Tart (see page 158), this rich, buttery, dried fruit tart is delightful served cold with a cup of tea, or warm with a dollop of thick cream for pudding.

This recipe is my adaptation of one from chefs Paul McCrindle and Angela MacKenzie at Peebles Hydro Hotel, where it is served for afternoon tea.

Serves 6–8
75g/3oz butter, melted
175g/6oz dark muscovado sugar
2 large free-range eggs, beaten
2 teaspoons white wine vinegar
225g/8oz mixed sultanas, currants
and raisins
110g/4oz walnuts, roughly chopped

For the pastry:
225g/8oz plain flour, sifted
150g/5oz butter, diced

To make the pastry, place the flour and butter in a food processor and process briefly, then add about 1 tablespoon of cold water – enough to bind – and process again. Bring the mixture together with your hands and wrap in clingfilm, then chill well. Roll out and use to line a 23cm/9in tart tin. Prick the base and chill well again.

Preheat the oven to 190°C/375°F/Gas 5. Line the pastry case with foil, fill with baking beans and bake for 15 minutes. Remove the foil and beans and bake for another 5 minutes, then remove the pastry case from the oven. Reduce the temperature to 180°C/350°F/Gas 4.

Beat together the melted butter and sugar, then add the eggs and vinegar. Stir well, then mix in the fruit and nuts. Tip this mixture into the part-baked pastry case and bake for 30 minutes, until set. You might need to cover the tart loosely with foil during the last 10 minutes or so to prevent the dried fruit burning. Remove from the oven and leave to cool, then cut into wedges to serve.

Potato Scones

Known more commonly as tattie scones, these girdle scones are often served for breakfast or tea. Sometimes I add about 25g/1oz grated Cheddar to the mixture and serve them with a bowl of broth or lentil soup for lunch. They are best eaten as soon as they are made (leftovers can be toasted the next day) but they can also be made in advance, then loosely wrapped in foil and reheated in a low oven.

Makes 8
1 large floury potato
(e.g. Maris Piper, King Edward
or Pentland Dell),
weighing about 250g/9oz
25g/1oz unsalted butter
50g/2oz plain flour
½ teaspoon salt
¼ teaspoon baking powder
a little butter for the girdle

Peel the potato, cut it into chunks and cook in boiling water until tender, then drain well. Using a potato masher, mash the potato with the butter. Now weigh it: you need about 200g/7oz mash.

Sift the flour, salt and baking powder into a bowl. While the mash is still warm, stir it into the flour and combine well to make a dough. Using lightly floured hands, gently shape the dough into 2 balls, then turn them on to a lightly floured surface. Roll out gently with a rolling pin to form 2 circles about 5mm/¼in thick. Cut each circle into quarters and prick all over with a fork.

Heat the girdle (or a large heavy frying pan) to medium-hot, smear over a little butter with a wad of kitchen paper then, once hot, transfer 4 scones to it with a large spatula or fish slice. Cook for about 3–4 minutes on each side, until golden brown. Transfer to a wire rack to cool slightly before spreading with a little butter and eating warm.

Fochabers Gingerbread

This is a rich, fruited gingerbread made with beer. No one is quite clear why the name Fochabers is associated with it but presumably it was originally made by someone from Fochabers, a town near Elgin in Moray, in the north-east of Scotland. Just like Orkney Broonie (see page 152) this is a cake that keeps well, wrapped in foil in a cake tin. It is a good choice for fireside teas in the middle of winter or for hearty picnics in the hills, preceded by the obligatory Thermos of soup.

Makes 1 Loaf

175g/6oz butter, softened
175g/6oz light muscovado sugar
3 heaped tablespoons black treacle
1 large free-range egg, beaten
300g/10½ oz plain flour, sifted
50g/2oz ground almonds
50g/2oz raisins
50g/2oz currants
1 teaspoon ground ginger
1 teaspoon mixed spice
1 rounded teaspoon bicarbonate of soda
125ml/4fl oz beer

Preheat the oven to 150°C/300°F/Gas 2. Cream the butter and sugar together, either in a mixer or by hand. Heat the treacle very gently until melted, then tip it into the bowl, add the egg and mix together. Stir in the flour, ground almonds, dried fruit, spices and bicarbonate of soda. Once everything is well mixed, stir in the beer and combine thoroughly. Tip into a buttered, base-lined 1kg/2¼lb loaf tin and bake for about 1½ hours, covering loosely with foil for the last half hour or so to prevent burning. Begin to test for readiness after 1¼ hours, by inserting a cocktail stick or skewer into the centre: it should come out clean. Transfer to a wire rack and leave to cool, then turn out of the tin. Wrap in foil once completely cold.

Black Bun

In our house at Hogmanay there were some things that never changed. The home-made blackcurrant cordial might have been replaced by Advocaat and lemonade as we became older, but there was always the tall, dark man (my father) at the door at midnight with a piece of coal as the 'first-foot' of the year; and there was always black bun – rich, heavy and dense – served alongside the plate of shortbread with wedges of Cheddar cheese and sultana or cherry cake. Black bun was perfect for soaking up the copious amounts of whisky proffered at every household ('One more dram before you go'). And our house was not unique. Black bun and 'shortie' were *de rigueur* everywhere, as we did the rounds of neighbours' houses, first-footing until the wee small hours.

Black bun was supposedly the original Twelfth Night cake eaten in Scotland, before it became known as 'Scotch Christmas bun' during the first half of the nineteenth century: there is a recipe for one in Meg Dodds' book of 1829. It was traditionally a spiced fruit mixture encased in bread dough but the dough gradually gave way to a lighter shortcrust pastry case. According to Catherine Brown, it seems the term Scotch Christmas Bun had disappeared by around 1914 and the name black bun seems to have been used from the late 1920s.

Serves 12–16

450g/1lb raisins
600g/1¼lb currants
110g/4oz whole blanched almonds,
 roughly chopped
50g/2oz walnuts, roughly chopped
150g/5oz plain flour, sifted
75g/3oz caster sugar
1 teaspoon ground allspice
1 teaspoon ground ginger
1 teaspoon ground cinnamon
½ teaspoon cream of tartar
½ teaspoon baking powder
2 tablespoons whisky
about 4 tablespoons milk

For the pastry:
275g/10oz plain flour, sifted
½ teaspoon baking powder
juice and grated zest of 1 lemon
150g/5oz unsalted butter, diced
beaten egg, to glaze

For the pastry, sift the flour and baking powder into a bowl and stir in the lemon zest. Rub in the butter, then add the lemon juice and 3–4 tablespoons cold water – enough to bind to a stiff dough. Turn out on to a lightly floured board and roll out thinly. Use two-thirds to line a buttered, square 23cm/9in cake tin. Roll out the remaining pastry to fit as a lid, then cover and chill both the lid and the case for half an hour or so.

Preheat the oven to 140°C/275°F/Gas 1. For the filling, mix everything together except the whisky and milk (I do this with my hands, which is easier). Then add the whisky and enough milk to moisten the mixture. Turn into the pastry case and press down well.

Dampen the edges of the pastry and place the rolled-out pastry lid on top. Press together the edges to seal, then cut off any excess pastry. Prick all over with a fork. Using a very thin skewer, prick right through to the base of the tin: 6–8 pricks altogether. Brush the surface with beaten egg, reserving a little. Place in the oven and bake for 2–2¼ hours, until golden brown on top. Glaze with the remaining egg after 1 hour.

Cool in the tin for at least 2 hours, then carefully decant on to a wire rack and leave to cool completely. Wrap in foil and store in an airtight container for up to 4 months.

shivery bites and sweeties 10

A shivery bite is just that — a bite of something delicious while you are shivering. In my parents' day, going for a swim at Dundee Swimming Baths was the highlight of many youngsters' weeks. (Oh, that the young nowadays revelled in such simple pleasures.) After swimming in the exceedingly chilly waters and drying off in unheated changing rooms, there was no way you wouldn't have been shivering. And so the shivery bite would sustain you through chattering teeth as you left the baths to face the icy blast coming directly off the River Tay.

Also known as chattery or chattering piece or chitterin bite in other areas of Scotland, it was essential fodder to warm you up and comfort you as you gradually thawed out. The type of food brought by children as shivery bites varied enormously. Favourites in my parents' day were Abernethy biscuits (and the not dissimilar Heckle biscuits), jam sandwiches, treacle toffee and apples. But when it was really cold, a roll filled with a sausage — especially square Lorne sausage — was a great treat. In my childhood, it might have been digestive biscuits sandwiched together with butter, or a butterie with cheese. Of course, children were soon simply given money to buy crisps or chocolate from the machines at the Baths: not quite as interesting, but a shivery bite nonetheless.

There are also 'sweeties' in this chapter. And what delights we could buy at the many sweetie shops throughout Scotland, from gobstoppers and tablet to curlie-murlies, glessies and teuch Jeans. Sadly, many of these old-fashioned sweets are dying out, but one thing is for sure: Scotland's famous sweet tooth is not. You might not have thought of making sweets before, but why not try one of my childhood favourites: tablet, treacle toffee or puff candy. Just be sure to brush your teeth afterwards.

Treacle Toffee

My Granny Anderson's treacle toffee recipe from her 1947 handwritten recipe book said simply to boil everything together for 15 minutes until crisp. She used milk instead of water. And in the ingredients list after the sugar and treacle, she wrote, '¼lb margarine (if not 2oz)' – whatever that means!

So I have changed her recipe a little and given rather more explicit instructions so that, if you have never made toffee before, you will feel confident. It might not be good for the teeth but I happen to love it.

Makes about 30 pieces
450g/1lb golden granulated sugar
225g/8oz black treacle (the easiest way to measure it is to pour out half a 450g/1lb tin)
75g/3oz butter
1 teaspoon white vinegar
150ml/5fl oz water

Place everything in a heavy-based saucepan. Stirring often, heat gently until the sugar dissolves and the butter melts. Then increase the heat and bring to the boil. Boil, stirring occasionally, for about 10 minutes or until a little of the mixture, when dropped into a cup of cold water, forms hard threads that bend without breaking. If you have a sugar thermometer, it should register 138°C/280°F.

Pour into a well-buttered 20–23cm/8–9in square baking tin and leave to cool. Cut into pieces when half set, then remove from the tin as best you can once cold.

Tablet

The scene is a large garden somewhere in Scotland on a warm summer afternoon, circa 1965. The occasion is the church garden fête. I remember queuing up (probably in my best cotton frock) at the cake and candy stall with my 3d to buy a bar of tablet before the fête had even been opened. And I was not alone. Tablet, neatly wrapped in waxed paper, was first to sell out at any fête, and the people in the queue stretching past the bric-a-brac and tombola stalls invariably ignored the lady in the big hat who was officially opening the fête, as they politely attempted to edge up the queue a little more.

These days, when invited to help at my church fair or coffee morning, I am often asked to help on the cake and candy stall. It might be inside a hall instead of outside on rolling lawns, but the spirit is the same. The tablet is always first to go – and there is never enough.

Almost unknown south of the border, tablet is one of Scotland's oldest types of confectionery. It is rather like fudge with a bite to it. Marion Lochhead refers to it in her book, *The Scots Household in the Eighteenth Century*: 'Barley-sugar, tablet, crokain [from the French *croquant* = crunchy] are all old and honourable Scots confections. Tablet might be made simply by boiling a pound of sugar in two gills of water until it candied; with cinnamon or ginger added for flavouring.' By 1929, when F. Marian McNeill wrote her book, milk had been added, for her recipe requires granulated sugar, thin cream or milk and flavouring. For the latter, she suggests cinnamon, coconut, fig, ginger, lemon, orange, peppermint, walnut or vanilla.

Having been brought up on plain tablet, I like it with just the merest hint of vanilla, pure and simple. If ever there was a childhood memory to evoke happy thoughts of sunshine, laughter and lush green gardens, it is an indulgent bite of tablet. I leave the rather more rarefied confections such as madeleines to Proust.

Makes 16–20 bars
125g/4½oz unsalted butter
1kg/2¼lb golden granulated sugar
300ml/10fl oz full-fat milk
a pinch of salt
200g/7oz tin of condensed milk
1 teaspoon pure vanilla essence

Place the butter in a large heavy-based saucepan (only a reliable pan should be used, otherwise the tablet mixture will stick) and melt over a low heat. Add the sugar, milk and salt and heat gently until the sugar has dissolved, stirring occasionally. Bring to the boil and simmer over a fairly high heat for 8–10 minutes, stirring often (and making sure you get into all the corners with your wooden spoon).

Add the condensed milk, stir well, then simmer for 8–10 minutes, stirring constantly. The mixture should bubble, but not too fiercely. After 8 minutes, test if it is ready. It should have reached the 'soft ball' stage, which means that when you drop a little of the mixture into a cup of very cold water, it will form a soft ball that you can pick up between your fingers. On a sugar thermometer, it should read 115°C/240°F.

Remove from the heat at once and add the vanilla (or other flavourings). Using an electric hand-held beater, beat at medium speed for 4–5 minutes, just until you feel the mixture begin to stiffen a little and become ever so slightly grainy. You can, of course, do this by hand but it will take at least 10 minutes and it is hard work! Pour immediately into a buttered 23 x 33cm/9 x 13in swiss roll tin and leave to cool. Mark into squares or oblongs when it is almost cold. When completely cold, remove and store in an airtight tin or wrap the pieces individually in waxed paper.

Chocolate Shortbread Truffles

Be sure to use either home-made or good-quality bought all-butter shortbread for these delicious truffles, which are wonderful served with post-prandial coffee or liqueurs.

Makes 24
250g/9oz good-quality dark chocolate
(55–70 per cent cocoa solids)
100g/3½oz unsalted butter
100g/3½oz shortbread,
crushed to crumbs
1 tablespoon whisky or Drambuie
2 tablespoons cocoa powder, sifted

Melt the chocolate and butter together over a low heat, then stir in the shortbread and whisky or Drambuie and mix thoroughly. Transfer to a shallow bowl and leave to cool, then chill for a couple of hours to firm up.

Using a teaspoon, spoon out some of the mixture and form into balls with the palms of your hands. At first it will seem hard, but it will soon soften up with the heat of your hands. Place the cocoa powder in a small bowl and roll each ball in this, then place on a board while you make the rest. The truffles will keep for a few days in an airtight tin.

Raggy Biscuits

Raggy biscuits are just that: ragged around the edges. They date back to the days before biscuit cutters. Although they are a speciality of Fife, I also found them in the Breadalbane Bakery in Aberfeldy, where they are known as raggie (sic) teas, rather like Rich Tea biscuits, as they are often eaten with a cup of tea. Raggy biscuits are now also eaten with cheese, since they are not too sweet. They have a lovely crisp texture and keep well.

In bakeries a special stamp with 'prickles' or tiny spikes is used to produce the distinctive 'prickled' appearance of the biscuits, which prevents them blistering during baking. At home this can be done with the tines of a fork.

Makes 20–24
275g/10oz self-raising flour, sifted
50g/2oz plain flour, sifted
75g/3oz golden caster sugar
110g/4oz butter, softened
a pinch of salt

Preheat the oven to 180°C/350°F/Gas 4. Put the flours into a food processor or mixer (or into a mixing bowl), add the sugar, butter and salt and process briefly until the mixture resembles breadcrumbs. Add 125–150ml (4–5fl oz) cold water and mix to a dough. (Or do everything by hand: rub the fat into the flour, stir in the sugar, then add enough water to combine.)

Divide the dough into small balls. Flatten these slightly, then fold in the edges irregularly. Then turn them over and flatten again with a rolling pin. The edges should be nicely ragged – if not, tease some of the dough out to make them look less regular. They should be about 5mm/¼in thick. Any thicker and they will still taste good but will not be as crisp. Place on 2 greased baking trays, prick all over with a fork and bake for 18–20 minutes, until pale golden brown. Transfer to a wire rack. As they cool they will crisp up.

Abernethy Biscuits

My father remembers eating Abernethy biscuits as a shivery bite after emerging from the freezing cold waters of Dundee Swimming Baths. Opened in the early 1930s, the baths were filled with salt water, filtered from the River Tay.

The biscuits are easy to make – and even easier to consume. My father ate them plain, or sometimes with butter and cheese. Some recipes include a teaspoon of caraway seeds.

Makes 20–24
225g/8oz plain flour,
1 teaspoon baking powder
75g/3oz butter, diced
75g/3oz golden caster sugar
1 large free-range egg, beaten
about 50ml/2fl oz milk

Preheat the oven to 180°C/350°F/Gas 4. Sift the flour and baking powder into a bowl, then rub in the butter until the mixture resembles breadcrumbs. Stir in the sugar, then add the beaten egg and enough milk to form a stiff dough that you can bring together with your hands. Turn it on to a floured surface and roll out to about 5mm/¼in thick. Cut out into rounds with a 5–6cm/2–2½in cutter. Place on a buttered baking sheet, prick all over with a fork and bake for 12–15 minutes or until pale golden brown. Transfer to a wire rack to cool and firm up.

Millionaire's Shortbread

This is definitely a more modern shivery bite. But it was a great treat for me as a child, since I have always loved everything to do with toffee, caramel and fudge. I like to include chocolate chunks in the shortbread base to add even more texture and taste. If you can find Argentinian dulce de leche, then it means you don't have to boil up a can of condensed milk for a couple of hours, as we had to do in the good old days.

Makes 24 squares
400g/14oz tin of condensed milk (or
450g/1lb jar of Argentinian dulce de leche)
250g/9oz good-quality milk or plain
chocolate

For the base:
300g/10½oz slightly salted butter,
softened
175g/6oz golden caster sugar
150g/5oz good-quality milk or plain
chocolate, chopped into small pieces
225g/8oz plain flour, sifted
110g/4oz semolina

If you are using condensed milk for the filling, start the day before: place the unopened tin in a deep pan with a lid and cover with water. Bring to the boil, cover and cook over a medium heat for 2 hours, then remove the tin from the water and leave overnight to cool down completely.

Preheat the oven to 150°C/300°F/Gas 2. For the base, cream the butter and sugar together until light and fluffy – I do this with an electric beater for 2–3 minutes. Stir in the chopped chocolate, then fold in the flour and semolina. Combine gently then tip into a greased 23 x 33cm/9 x 13in swiss roll tin. The mixture will look a complete mess so, using floured hands, press it into the tin to even the surface, then prick all over with a fork. Bake for 40 minutes, until firm around the edges and pale golden brown. Remove from the oven and leave to cool in the tin for about 30 minutes.

Open the tin of condensed milk (which will now be caramel) and pour it over the shortbread base (or use the dulce de leche, which you may want to warm up a little in the microwave first). Melt the chocolate and pour it over the caramel, spreading it all over. Once it has set a little, but before it is hard, cut into squares. Remove from the tin when completely cold.

Puff Candy

When I was little, my mother used to send me off to the local dairy for shopping. I used to love Moffats Dairy, as there were large trays of puff candy for sale beside the cheese, cream and butter. I was allowed to buy some of this golden confection and remember devouring it on the way home. Also called honeycomb, puff candy is just like a Crunchie bar without the chocolate coating. It is also what New Zealanders use in their wonderful hokey-pokey ice-cream. In fact you can make that with this recipe: just bash the puff candy up into small pieces and fold them into softened good-quality vanilla ice-cream: 1 litre/1¾ pints for this amount.

Makes a 18cm/7in tray
4 heaped tablespoons granulated sugar
2 heaped tablespoons golden syrup
1 teaspoon bicarbonate of soda

Put the sugar and syrup in a heavy-based pan and allow to dissolve slowly over a low heat, stirring well. Increase the heat to medium and bring to the boil, stirring constantly. Once you see bubbles, reduce the heat slightly and simmer for about 3 minutes, still stirring constantly, until it is a rich golden brown. Do not allow it to become too dark or it will have a slightly bitter flavour. It should be the colour of a Crunchie bar.

Remove from the heat and stir in the bicarbonate of soda until the mixture froths up. Tip immediately into a well-buttered, base-lined 18cm/7in shallow baking tin. It is really important to butter the base and sides or the mixture will stick. Leave to cool completely. To remove, cut into large pieces or bash out the pieces with the end of a rolling pin. Eat plain, or melt some chocolate (I use half milk, half plain) and dip the puff candy pieces into it. Set on a board to cool.

Bibliography

Ena Baxter:
Scottish Cookbook
(Johnston & Bacon, 1974)

John Beatty: *Sula, the Seabird-hunters of Lewis*
(Michael Joseph, 1992)

Catherine Brown:
Scottish Cookery
(Richard Drew Publishing, 1989)

Catherine Brown:
A Year in the Scots Kitchen
(Neil Wilson Publishing, 1996)

Laura Mason & Catherine Brown:
Traditional Foods of Britain
(Prospect Books, 1999)

Hamish Whyte & Catherine Brown:
A Scottish Feast
(Argyll Publishing, 1996)

Lady Clark of Tillypronie:
The Cookery Book of Lady Clark of Tillypronie 1909
(Southover Press, 1994)

Elizabeth Craig:
What's Cooking in Scotland?
(Oliver and Boyd Ltd, 1965)

Clarissa Dickson Wright:
The Haggis, A Little History
(Appletree Press Ltd, 1996)

Clarissa Dickson Wright with Henry Crichton-Stuart:
Hieland Foodie
(NMS Publishing, 1999)

Mistress Margaret Dods: *Cook and Housewife's Manual 1829*
(Roster Ltd, 1988)

B. Faujas de Saint-Fond: *A Journey through England and Scotland to the Hebrides in 1784, Vols 1 & 2*

Theodora Fitzgibbon:
A Taste of Scotland
(Pan Books, 1971)

Willie Fulton: *The Hebridean Kitchen*
(Buidheann-foillseachaidh nan Eilian an Iar, 1978)

Denis Girard: *Cassell's New French-English English-French Dictionary*
(Cassell, 1962)

I. F. Grant: *Highland Folk Ways*
(Birlinn Ltd, 1997)

Peter Irvine: *Scotland the Best*
(Mainstream, 1996)

Samuel Johnson & James Boswell:
A Journey to the Western Islands of Scotland & The Journal of a Tour to the Hebrides (1773)
(Penguin Books, 1984)

Mark Kurlansky: *Cod*
(Vintage, 1999)

Robbie and Nora Kydd:
Growing Up in Scotland
(Polygon, 1998)

G. W. Lockhart:
The Scot and His Oats
(Luath Press, 1983)

Hollier-Larousse:
Larousse Gastronomique
(Paul Hamlyn Ltd, 1961)

Marion Lochhead:
The Scots Household in the Eighteenth Century
(The Moray Press, 1948)

Peter Martin:
A Life of James Boswell
(Weidenfeld & Nicolson, 1999)

W. M. Mathew:
Keiller's of Dundee
(Abertay Historical Society, 1998)

F. Marian McNeill:
The Scots Kitchen (1929)
(The Mercat Press, 1993)

F. Marian McNeill:
Recipes from Scotland (1946)
(Gordon Wright Publishing, 1994)

Gladys Menhinick:
Grampian Cookbook
(The Mercat Press, 1993)

Grace Mulligan:
Dundee Kitchen
(David Winter & Son Ltd, 1991)

Christina Noble:
The Story of Loch Fyne Oysters
(Oyster Ideas Ltd, 1993)

Judi Paterson:
The Scottish Cook
(Birlinn Ltd, 1995)

Judi Paterson:
Scottish Home Cooking
(Lindsay Publications, 1995)

Jenni Simmons:
A Shetland Cookbook
(The Shetland Times, 1978)

Tom Steel:
The Life and Death of St Kilda
(HarperCollins, 1994)

Janet Warren:
A Feast of Scotland
(Lomond Books, 1997)

Dorothy Wordsworth: *Recollections of a Tour Made in Scotland in 1803*
(The Mercat Press, 1981)

R. L. Stevenson:
Kidnapped (1886)
(Bloomsbury Books, 1994)

Eileen Wolf:
Recipes from the Orkney Islands
(Gordon Wright Publishing, 1978)

Useful Addresses and Mail Order

Aberdeen and Grampian Tourist Board
27 Albyn Place
Aberdeen AB10 1YL
Tel: 01224 288800

Angus and City of Dundee Tourist Board
21 Castle Street
Dundee DD1 3AA
Tel: 01382 527527

Argyll, The Isles, Loch Lomond, Stirling, Trossachs Tourist Board
Old Town Jail
St John Street
Stirling FK8 1EA
Tel: 01786 445222

Ayrshire and Arran Tourist Board
Burns House
Burns Statue Square
Ayr KA7 1UP
Tel: 01292 262555

Dumfries and Galloway Tourist Board
64 Whitesands
Dumfries DG1 2RS
Tel: 01387 245550

Edinburgh and Lothians Tourist Board
4 Rothesay Terrace
Edinburgh EH3 7RY
Tel: 0131 473 3600

Greater Glasgow and Clyde Valley Tourist Board
11 George Square
Glasgow G2 1DY
Tel: 0141 204 4480

The Highlands and Scotland Tourist Board
Peffery House
Strathpeffer
IV14 9HA
Tel: 01997 421160

Kingdom of Fife Tourist Board
Haig House
Balgonie Road
Markinch KY7 6AQ
Tel: 01592 750066

Orkney Tourist Board
6 Broad Street
Kirkwall
Orkney KW15 1NX
Tel: 01856 872856

Perthshire Tourist Board
West Mill Street
Perth PH1 5QP
Tel: 01738 627958

Scottish Borders Tourist Board
Shepherds Mills
Whinfield Road
Selkirk TD7 5DT
Tel: 01750 20555

Shetland Islands Tourism
Market Cross
Lerwick
Shetland ZE1 0LU
Tel: 01595 693434

Western Isles Tourist Board
4 South Beach
Stornoway
Isle of Lewis HS1 2XY
Tel: 01851 701818

Most of the following companies will supply mail order:

Arbroath smokies
R. R. Spink and Sons,
33 Seagate,
Arbroath DD11 1BJ.
Tel: 01241 872023.

Ayrshire bacon
Ramsay of Carluke,
22 Mount Stewart Street,
Carluke ML8 5ED.
Tel: 01555 772277.
www.ramsayofcarluke.co.uk

Beef
Donald Russell,
Harlaw Road,
Inverurie, Aberdeenshire,
AB51 4FR.
Tel: 01467 629666.
www.donaldrussell.co.uk

(Stornoway) black pudding and Hebridean lamb
Charles Macleod Butcher,
Ropewood Park,
Stornoway HS1 2LB.
Tel: 01851 702445.
www.charlesmacleod.co.uk

Black pudding (and baby pudding)
John Henderson Butcher,
67 High Street, Kircaldy.
Tel: 01592 260980.

Butteries
The Seafield Bakery,
11 Seafield Street,
Cullen AB56 4SG.
Tel: 01542 840512.

Aitkens Bakery,
Glenbervie Road, Aberdeen.
Tel: 01224 877768.

Dried carragheen, dulse and beremeal flour
Real Foods,
37 Broughton Street, Edinburgh.
Tel: 0131 557 1911.

Dundee cake
Goodfellow & Steven Bakers,
81 Gray Street,
Broughty Ferry DD5 2BQ.
Tel: 01382 730181.

Forfar bridies
McLaren Bakers,
Market Street, Forfar.
Tel: 01307 463315.

Fresh herbs
Scotherbs,
Kingswell,
Longforgan, near Dundee,
DD2 5HJ.
Tel: 01382 360642.
www.scotherbs.com

Game and beef
George Bower Butcher,
75 Raeburn Place, Edinburgh.
Tel: 0131 332 3469.

Game
Highland Game Ltd,
Baird Avenue,
Dundee DD2 3XA.
Tel: 01382 827088.

Haggis, black and white pudding
Macsween of Edinburgh,
Bilston Glen,
Loanhead EH20 9LZ.
Tel: 0131 440 2555.
www.macsween.co.uk

Holyrood tarts and Aberfeldy whisky cake
Breadalbane Bakery, Aberfeldy.
Tel: 01887 820481.

Lorne sausage, white puddings and Scotch pies
Robertson's the Butcher,
234 Brook Street, Broughty Ferry.
Tel: 01382 739277.

Oatmeal
Aberfeldy Water Mill,
Mill Street,
Aberfeldy, Perthshire PH15 2BG.
Tel: 01887 820803.

Oysters and kippers
Loch Fyne Smokehouse,
Ardkinglas, Argyll.
Tel: 01499 600217.
www.loch-fyne.com

Potted hough, haggis and meat roll
Forsyths Butchers,
21 Eastgate, Peebles EH45 8AD.
Tel: 01721 720833.

Puggy buns, raggy biscuits and Hedderwick buns
Adamson's Bakery,
Pittenweem.
Tel: 01333 311336.

Reestit (reested) mutton and sassermeat
James Smith Butchers,
177 Commercial Street,
Lerwick, Shetland.
Tel: 01595 692355.

Shortbread
Shortbread House of Edinburgh,
14 Broompark EH5 1RS.
Tel: 0131 552 0381.

Smoked salmon (hot and cold smoke), salt herring, smoked haddock and finnan haddock
George Armstrong,
80 Raeburn Place EH4.
Tel: 0131 315 2033.

Ken Watmough,
29 Thistle Street,
Aberdeen.
Tel 01224 640321.

(Farmed) Venison
Fletchers Fine Foods, Reediehill
Farm, Auchtermuchty, KY14 7HS.
Tel: 01337 828369.
www.fletcherscotland.co.uk

Index

Note: Page references in bold type indicate recipes; those in italics indicate illustrations.